FIFTH EDITION

Success at the Enquiry Desk

Successful enquiry answering – every time

Tim Buckley Owen

facet publishing

© Tim Buckley Owen 1996, 1997, 1998, 2000, 2003, 2006

Published by
Facet Publishing
7 Ridgmount Street
London WC1E 7AE

Facet Publishing is wholly owned by CILIP: the Chartered Institute of Library and Information Professionals.

First published by Library Association Publishing in the *Successful LIS Professional* series, edited by Sheila Pantry 1996
First revised edition 1997
Second revised edition 1998
Third edition 2000
Fourth edition 2003, reprinted 2004
Fifth edition 2006

British Library Cataloguing in Publication Data
A catalogue record for this book is available from the British Library.

ISBN-10: 1-85604-600-1
ISBN-13: 978-1-85604-600-8

Typeset in 11/14 pt Minion and Myriad by Facet Publishing.
Printed and made in Great Britain by MPG Books Ltd, Bodmin, Cornwall.

Contents

FIFTH EDITION

Success at the Enquiry Desk

Introduction

Every time I've come to revise this book I've started by saying: 'There's never been a better time to be in the library and information profession'. It's still true; but demonstrating how you can add value as an information professional becomes an ever greater challenge. As internet use becomes more and more widespread, the skill stakes have been raised. Everyone's an expert searcher these days – or so they think – and there is acute pressure on us as information professionals to perform ever more effectively.

Should we fear this? Certainly not! For years people in this profession bemoaned the fact that decision-makers didn't recognize the value of information or appreciate the special knowledge and skills that we as library and information professionals could bring to bear in managing and exploiting it. Well, now they do recognize the value of information, and it's up to us to ensure that they also understand that we can add to that value even more.

There's a saying amongst theatrical folk: amateurs rehearse to make sure everything goes right; professionals rehearse to make sure nothing goes wrong. It's spot on as far as enquiry work is concerned; lots of things can go wrong, and it's up to us to know where the pitfalls lie, to anticipate problems and avoid them. DIY searching tools are available to everyone now. So our job as professionals is, firstly, to use those tools more effectively than the amateurs can and, secondly, to bring in more efficient specialist tools when the DIY ones show that they're not up to the job. How do we find out what those tools are? How do we use them effectively? That's what this book is all about.

It's an introduction to techniques that can help you deal with enquiries on any subject, whether or not there are any publications about it. These techniques make use of the web where appropriate, but they meld it with other sources, both printed and electronic, for maximum value. The techniques work equally effectively for enquiries on any subject – social, economic, cultural, scientific or technological. Certainly we need to have some key information sources always at our fingertips, but that's not fundamentally what enquiry answering is about.

In essence, successful enquiry answering is about applied common sense, shared experience and exercise of the imagination. As more and more emphasis is laid on information handling skills in formal education, and growing numbers of people engage in self-directed lifelong learning using the internet, then techniques such as these will become more widespread across the population as a whole. What we professionals need to do is systematize these techniques, learn from our experience, and keep our skills in the peak of condition at all times. We need to attend training courses and briefing sessions. We need to gain qualifications that will provide evidence of our competence to our enquirers and to potential employers – qualifications such as those offered by CILIP: the Chartered Institute of Library and Information Professionals. In short, we need to demonstrate the commitment that people expect of professionals.

One thing the internet has done is to increase dramatically the range of opportunities for professional enquiry answering activity. This is no longer the exclusive preserve of the person sitting in a book-lined room – although, as this book will demonstrate, print on paper remains a remarkably effective medium for storing and retrieving information. Nevertheless, the extraordinary technological developments of the last decade or so have meant that we are just as likely to be working in a call centre – using only a few printed sources and largely reliant on electronic information media. Or we might even be constantly on the move, with only a laptop and a mobile phone as our means of access to the world of knowledge that we need to do our job.

Nor should we assume any more that we have to rely exclusively on material that's in the public domain: printed publications, online databases, other public enquiry services. We're just as likely to be exploiting unpublished sources as well: internal records and datasets, even the knowledge in people's heads. Increasingly, this job is not simply about providing support to decision-makers, but about adding value in our own right. It's not merely about seeking out the best sources for the job, but about exploiting them and turning them into new information sources, fit for the purpose. It's about going the extra mile; years ago we may simply have been lookers-up, but now, increasingly, we need to be publishers as well.

This fifth edition includes a new chapter – on how to set up and develop your own information service in a new job. It also takes into account all sorts of technological developments that have emerged since the fourth edition was published three years ago – blogs, wikis, RSS feeds, and so on. But, more than anything else, it draws upon the comments of the many participants who have taken part in my enquiry handling courses based on this book. Their experience, their insight and their view of what it is like to run an information service in the twenty-first century have been invaluable to me in revising the book, and I am profoundly grateful to them all.

It really is true; there has never been a better time to be in the information profession. But there's never been a more challenging time either. So you need to start somewhere, and I hope this book will help you grasp the basic principles of one of the world's most fascinating professions. After that, the opportunities are limited only by your own imagination.

Tim Buckley Owen

Five fundamentals of successful enquiry answering

It's all too easy for your mind to go completely blank when faced with the challenge of a new enquiry. If you can remember nothing else, try to keep these five fundamentals in mind. They'll help you get started, and keep you on track.

1 Never take an enquiry at face value, always ask a question back – because you never know where it may lead.
2 Start by imagining what the final answer will look like – that will help you focus on the best sources and delivery media for the job.
3 Jot down the search terms you're going to use in a structured hierarchy, not just a random list – that will help you search more efficiently and quickly.
4 If you can't find the answer, ask yourself who really needs to know this information – that should give you ideas for who to ask for help.
5 Make sure you always add value when presenting your answer – that will demonstrate your professionalism.

Nine steps to successful enquiry answering: the *Success at the Enquiry Desk* enquiry form

Enquiry forms come in all shapes and sizes. At their most basic, they may simply have somewhere to record the question and the enquirer's contact details, followed by a large blank space for you to use as you wish. More complex forms may require you to record your search strategy, or even include suggestions for sources you could try. A growing number of library and information services are using electronic enquiry recording – either by developing their own systems based on a standard database package such as Microsoft Access, or by purchasing ready-made enquiry management packages. Networked, these can enable any member of staff to keep track of progress on enquiries and can facilitate collaborative enquiry answering; they can also provide an audit trail for charging purposes. At the oither extreme, some libraries and information units don't use forms at all, but rely on notebooks or even scrap paper.

Our enquiry form (on pages xvi and xvii) tries to give you as much help as possible. In nine steps, it takes you through the entire process, from recording the question to the final sign-off, when the enquiry has been answered successfully and you are considering what follow-up action it may require – recording a useful new reference source in your information file, for example, or a new website that you could add to your favourites for future use. We make sure that you analyse the enquiry accurately (step 3), and that you plan your search strategy properly (step 5). At steps 4 and 6, we make suggestions on possible sources and delivery media you could try – first the types of source that might be suitable, and then some actual titles. In fact, our enquiry form follows the structure of this book.

We've had to compress the form to fit it onto the book's small pages; you'd certainly need a lot more space for sections 6 and 7 than we allow here, for example. And what you see as a pair of facing pages would actually be the front and back if it were a paper form. If it were electronic, then the lists that you see on the second page would work very well as checkable pull-down menus. If you find it helpful as a model, then you may like to adapt it – in printed or electronic form – for use in your own library or information unit.

1 **QUESTION** (as much detail as possible)	2 **ENQUIRER DETAILS**
	Name:
	Organization:
	Address:
	Postcode:
	Tel:
Enquiry taken by:	Fax:
Deadline:	E-mail:
	Special contact instructions:

3 **ENQUIRY ANALYSIS**	4 **ENQUIRY TYPE**
	Focus
Who?	Broad: ❏ Narrow: ❏
	Dynamism
What?	Static: ❏ Dynamic: ❏
When?	**Complexity**
	Single issue: ❏ Multi-faceted: ❏
Where?	*(See over for possible types of source to use)*
Why?	**Viability**
	Can't be answered in-house: ❏
How?	Not available in a published source: ❏
What will the final answer look like?	**Who really needs to know this**?

5 SEARCH STRATEGY
Broader terms:

   ROOT TERMS:

     Narrower terms:

Related terms:

6 **SOURCES TRIED**	7 **SEARCH RESULTS**
(See over for possible starter sources)	

8 **ANSWER**	9 **SIGN-OFF**
	Enquiry completed by:
	Answer delivered by:
	Success…
	Complete: ❏ Partial: ❏ Compromise: ❏
	Enquiry referred to:
	Time taken to answer: ……..hrs ……. mins
	When completed:
	Delivered on time… Yes: ❏ No: ❏
	Reasons if late:
	Follow-up action (e.g. add new information or source to information file):

TYPES OF SOURCE TO CONSIDER (Section 4)

FOCUS
Broad
Entry in a general encyclopaedia
Chapter in a textbook
Complete textbook

Narrow
Entry in a special encyclopaedia
Index entry in a textbook
Special report
Journal article
Statistical table
Entry in a directory
Database record (online or portable)
Website or page

DYNAMISM
Static
Encyclopaedia or dictionary
Textbook
Selection of journal articles
Statistical time series
Directory
Database (portable or online)

Dynamic
Online news service (free or charged)
Online database (real-time or archival)
Teletext or audiotex
Press release
Current newspaper
Recent journal
Latest statistics

COMPLEXITY
Single issue
Printed source (if easy to find)
Specialist database (if hard to find)
Web search engine (last resort)

Multi-faceted
Specialist database (online or portable)
Web search engine (advanced search)

VIABILITY
Can't be answered in-house
Library or information unit guide
Nearby public or educational library
Online discussion list
Independent information professional

Not available in a published source
Specialist organization
Author of nearly relevant publication
Editor of relevant journal
Online discussion list
Independent information professional

POSSIBLE STARTER SOURCES (Section 6)

Identifying basic reference sources
Know it All, Find it Fast
The New Walford: Guide to Reference Resources
Current British Directories

Identifying and tracing books
British National Bibliography
LibWeb

Identifying journals and newspapers
Benn's Media
Willing's Press Guide

Tracing articles
Abstracts in New Technologies and Engineering
Applied Social Sciences Index and Abstracts
British Humanities Index

Tracing news items
BBC News Online: http://news.bbc.co.uk

Identifying and tracing statistics
Office for National Statistics: www.statistics.gov.uk
Annual Abstract of Statistics
Sources of Non-official UK Statistics

Comprehensive facts and figures
Whitaker's Almanac
UK… the Official Yearbook of the United Kingdom of
    Great Britain and Northern Ireland

Comprehensive events and dates
Keesing's Record of World Events
Annual Register

Comprehensive online archives
Dialog: www.dialog.com

Finding contacts for further information
Aslib Directory of Information Sources in the United
    Kingdom
Europa World of Learning
Hollis UK Public Relations Annual
Directory of British Associations
Councils, Committees and Boards
Centres, Bureaux and Research Institutes

Twenty-five multi-purpose reference sources you can't afford to ignore

Ever since you were a child at school, you've been looking things up – using encyclopaedias, dictionaries, phone books, recipe books, Who's Whos. By now you'll also be familiar with your own in-house catalogues and finding aids, including any internal information files that your colleagues may have compiled. You'll know about your collection of reference works, newspapers, journals or statistics, in both printed and electronic form, and you should have access to the internet. In other words, you already know a great deal about how to find information.

But for really successful enquiry work, there's a small core of more specialist reference sources that it's worth knowing about. Over the page you'll find a quick checklist of some of the most useful British ones and their international equivalents. Readers in other countries should be able to build up a list of their own equivalent publications as they gain more and more experience at enquiry answering. Finally, there's a full guide to all the reference sources listed here, with annotations, at the end of the book.

Most of these sources started as printed publications, but many are now also available electronically – via the web or possibly on CD-ROM. Some are web-only. Where possible, I have indicated in the guide to key reference sources when a source is also available in electronic form; *Know It All, Find It Fast* (number 1 in this list) will often give you this information as well. Access to official websites (government or international organizations) should be free, but on many other sites the information will be password-protected and available only on subscription at commercial prices. In some cases, though, you can buy information by credit card or through online payment services such as Paypal (www.paypal.com) on a pay-per-view basis.

You'll also find that there's no comprehensive guide to websites listed here. That's because virtually every one of these sources, and most others that you'll use as well, will include references to websites that can lead you to further information, organizations or contacts. As a general rule, it's far more efficient to find suitable websites by using a professionally edited source (such as any of those listed here) rather than a generic search engine. Websites that you find through a quality controlled source are far more likely to be quality controlled themselves, and hence reliable.

It's difficult to carry too many sources of this kind in your head – 25 seems a good number to start with. So try to become familiar with them (and their international equivalents); they'll get you started on a great many of the enquiries you'll have to deal with.

Twenty-five multi-purpose reference sources

Purpose	No	Source	International equivalents
Identifying basic reference sources	1 2 3	Know It All, Find It Fast The New Walford: Guide to Reference Resources Current British Directories	[Know It All, Find It Fast] [The New Walford: Guide to Reference Resources] Ulrich's Periodicals Directory
Identifying and tracing books	4 5	British National Bibliography LibWeb	British Library Integrated Catalogue [LibWeb] Amazon.com Global Books In Print Google Books Library Project
Identifying journals and newspapers	6 7	Benn's Media Willing's Press Guide	[Benn's] [Willing's] Ulrich's Periodicals Directory
Tracing articles	8 9 10	Abstracts In New Technologies and Engineering Applied Social Sciences Index and Abstracts British Humanities Index	Applied Science and Technology Index/Abstracts/full text General Science Index/Abstracts/full text Sociological Abstracts Social Sciences Index/Abstracts/full text Humanities Index/Abstracts/full text British Library Direct British Library Inside Emerald Insight IngentaConnect Sage Full Text Collections Wilson OmniFile Full Text Mega Edition
Tracing news items	11	BBC News Online: http://news.bbc.co.uk	[BBC News Online] Keesing's Record of World Events
Identifying and tracing statistics	12 13 14	Office for National Statistics: www.statistics.gov.uk Annual Abstract of Statistics Sources of Non-official UK Statistics	United Nations Statistics Division: http://unstats.un.org/unsd United Nations Statistical Yearbook Europe In Figures: Eurostat Yearbook World Marketing Data and Statistics on the Internet World Directory of Non-official Statistical Sources
Comprehensive facts and figures	15 16	Whitaker's Almanac UK… The Official Yearbook of the United Kingdom of Great Britain and Northern Ireland	Europa World Yearbook Statesman's Yearbook World Fact Book
Comprehensive events and dates	17 18	Keesing's Record of World Events Annual Register	[Keesing's Record of World Events] [Annual Register]
Comprehensive online archives	19	Dialog: www.dialog.com	[Dialog] Lexisnexis
Finding contacts for further information	20 21 22 23 24 25	Aslib Directory of Information Sources in the United Kingdom Europa World of Learning Hollis UK Public Relations Annual Directory of British Associations Councils, Committees and Boards Centres, Bureaux and Research Institutes	[Europa World of Learning] Hollis Europe Directory of European Professional and Learned Societies Encyclopaedia of Associations: International Organizations Europa Directory of International Organizations World Directory of Trade and Business Associations Yearbook of International Organizations

CHAPTER 1

What do you really want?

How to make sure you really understand the question

> **In this chapter you'll find out how to:**
>
> - avoid misunderstandings
> - ask the right questions
> - agree the task
> - find out how long you've got to do it.

There's a story told of a London taxi driver some years ago who picked up an American lady outside her hotel. There was a big Egyptology exhibition on at the British Museum at the time. 'Take me to Tutankhamun,' the lady drawled. So the cabbie did. Thirty minutes later he dropped her at a rather down-at-heel patch of open space in the south-west London suburbs, called Tooting Common.

It's an apocryphal tale, no doubt. But it does show the problems you can hit when dealing with what seems like the simplest of enquiries. Some of your queries will come orally, face-to-face. The possibilities for misunderstandings are endless – accent, articulation, assumptions, all can send you scurrying off in totally the wrong direction, wasting both your time and the enquirer's. With face-to-face enquiries, you are at least offered lots of clues; most of what we communicate is non-verbal, so you are able to glean what you can from facial expression, eye contact, body language. But you are deprived of these clues when your queries come in by phone, and you have even less to go on when they arrive in written form – by e-mail, fax or post. So the first task has to be: no matter how your enquiry comes in, always make sure you understand the question.

Avoiding misunderstandings

Remember when you were doing your exams, and teachers and lecturers dinned into you the lesson 'read the whole paper first'? Well, it matters just as much here. Because, if you get it wrong, it'll be your fault no matter how unhelpful the enquirer has been. You are the professional, remember, and the enquirer is the amateur.

Just think of all the different types of enquirer you might meet, and the things that could go wrong as a result . . .

Type 1: The homophone victim

I'm looking for information on migration patterns in whales

means:

I'm looking for information on migration patterns in Wales

Type 2: The Chinese whisperer

I'm trying to find a song called When I would sing under the ocean

means:

I'm trying to find a song called When I was king of the Beotians

Type 3: The malapropist

Do you have the Electrical Register?

means:

Do you have the electoral register?

Type 4: The generalist

Do you have any books on retailing?

means:

What is Marks & Spencer's current pretax profit?

Type 5: The know-all
Where do you keep the New Scientist?

means:

I think I saw an article recently about the research that's been done into the health effects of radiation, both from artificial and natural sources, and who's doing it. I don't want to appear ignorant so I'm just going to ask for the latest New Scientist, *which is where I think I saw it. [In fact, the article appeared in* Nature, *and was published months ago.]*

Type 6: The muddler
Have you got any books on Kew Gardens? That's to say, something on the Crystal Palace, if you can manage it. What would be really helpful, actually, would be the index to the Illustrated London News. *Or, better still, a book on tropical fish.*

means:

I'm doing a project on the Westminster Aquarium.

Type 7: The obsessively secretive
Where's the catalogue?

means (after a lot of tactful questioning):

I know there have been reports in the papers that MPs have been accepting cash in return for asking Parliamentary questions, and that one paper has actually named names. I'm very concerned about this because my brother is an MP and he may be involved because he's been asking questions about immigration quotas and he's sponsored by the Strong & Moral Britain Association, which I think is associated with neo-fascist organizations. Can you confirm this, or let me know where its funding comes from? I really need to know because I'm about to become a governor of a school with a large number of Asian children – so I'd also like to find out what obligation there is on school governors to declare other interests, but I don't want to approach the school directly about this in case they start asking awkward questions.

Most of these are based on real enquiries, some are exaggerations. (The last one is almost a total fiction.) But they all pose real dangers. Rule number one of enquiry answering is that people almost never ask the question they really want to know the answer to.

Disgruntled and unconvinced enquirers

There are all sorts of reasons for this. They may not want to bother the staff. It's true, a big public or educational library can be a busy place. You can have people queuing up at the enquiry desk just when Maisie decides to go off for coffee. When you're under pressure, it's always a temptation to take an enquiry at face value and answer the question actually put to you. Resist it! You're almost certain to have a disgruntled customer returning to the enquiry desk before too long, and that's a waste of everybody's time, and really bad customer relations.

Equally alarming is the kind of enquirer who lacks confidence in your ability to answer the question. They'd sooner browse themselves, perhaps inefficiently, than risk having their time wasted by you. This kind of enquirer should be sending alarm signals both to you and to your boss. It probably means that they've had bad experiences before – either with your service or somewhere else. Either way, it's up to you to convince them, quickly, that you can help, even if you don't know anything about the subject they are interested in. This doesn't mean trying to pull the wool over their eyes – that's the worst possible tactic. You're bound to get found out, and you'll just reinforce the enquirer's scepticism. There are ways of being helpful, even if you haven't a clue what the enquirer is talking about.

Secretive enquirers and time-wasters

Then there are enquirers who just don't want anyone to know what they're doing. These can be the most infuriating kind. Despite your gentle persuasion, they resolutely refuse to disclose any information that might help you to help them. But you must suppress your urge to get annoyed. That will only make matters worse. They may have excellent reasons for not wanting to give anything away. It might be someone applying for a job with a big local firm who doesn't want their current employer to get wind of it. It might be an academic who doesn't want to be beaten to publication by a rival. Or would you want everyone to know that you were looking for addresses of HIV clinics?

Finally, there are time wasters – people who want to burden you with every tiny detail of their investigation, together with the complete life stories of all their sisters, cousins and aunts. Genealogical enquirers frequently fall into this category. You owe it to your other enquirers to steer this type to the point as quickly as possible. They'll try to persuade you that you can't possibly help them without a full understanding of their needs. They may genuinely believe this, or they may simply have time on their hands, and be looking for someone to talk to. Either way, you have to focus them, tactfully.

There are ways of dealing with all these types. You'll need to be approachable, reassuring, discreet and tactful. This is relatively easy to do face-to-face, but is more difficult on the phone, because you're not giving the enquirer any visual clues. One thing that does work is to smile when you're on the phone; it can work wonders with a suspicious or hostile enquirer! What you really need to do, though, is to maintain what the police used to call an attitude of 'suspicious alertness'. You have to find out what you need to know by asking questions, and there are several different questioning techniques that you can employ. This is sometimes rather pretentiously referred to as 'the reference interview', but that implies a formality about the process that can be off-putting for the enquirer. It's really just a structured conversation, directed by you.

Asking the right questions

One of the most useful things you can learn to do in enquiry work is to get into the habit of always asking a supplementary question. Practise it in conversation until it becomes second nature. It can provide an enormous number of clues as to what your enquirer really wants – and can sometimes reveal something completely unexpected that can prevent you from darting off in the wrong direction. Here's a silly example: you're in the kitchen and you think your partner said, 'Have you got the time?' So you reply, 'Do you mean what time is it now or how long does it take to cook?' 'No, no,' your partner answers, 'Did you remember to buy the thyme?'

It's probably second nature to ask a supplementary question in conversation – face-to-face or on the phone – but you should also do it if at all possible with written enquiries as well. This can admittedly be awkward and time-consuming if you are responding to a fax or letter. But with enquiries that come in by e-mail, it's easy; you should look carefully at the wording and respond immediately, asking questions that will help you to help your enquirer better.

You need different kinds of questions for different situations, different techniques for dealing with each of the types of enquirer profiled above. Let's run through the techniques, and the situations in which you might use them.

Open questions

These invite the enquirer to supply further details without your specifying what additional information would be helpful. You might need to use an open question to deal with a type 4 enquirer (the generalist). Perhaps something like 'Are you interested in any particular aspect of retailing?' And it may be your only way forward with type 7 (the obsessively secretive) with a response like 'I could give you a hand if you can give me an idea of what subject you're interested in.' However, open questions do have the disadvantage of leaving far too many options open.

Closed questions

These force the enquirer to give you a yes/no answer. With type 5 (the know-all) you might be tempted to ask, 'Is it the current issue you're looking for?' But, if the know-all runs true to type, the answer will undoubtedly be 'Yes,' and you will have learned nothing. So you should use closed questions only when you are certain what the options are. For example, you could ask type 3 (the malapropist) 'Do you want the register for this area?' (see below – 'Who, What, When, Where, Why, How?').

Forced choice questions

These force the enquirer to choose between two alternatives only. The little kitchen sink drama above uses a forced choice question. Or you might ask a type 1 enquirer (the homophone victim), 'Do you mean the sea creatures or the country?' Forced choice questions can be very helpful – they immediately narrow the field in a way that is being firmly directed by you. But you have to learn to think quickly to come up with two really useful options. You sometimes have to be tactful with forced choice questions too. After all, it's perfectly clear to the *enquirer* what they want!

Multiple questions

These offer the enquirer a range of options to choose from. You'd use a multiple question when you're really not sure at all what the enquirer wants and you need to fish for ideas. An alternative might be to use an open question, but multiple-choice questions are likely to be much more useful, provided you can think quickly enough to come up with some sensible options. Instead of using an open question for type 4 (the generalist), you could try, 'Are you looking for information on retail management, shop design or location, market research, special types of retailer such as food or electrical goods shops – or even one particular retailer?' The only real problem with multiple questions is that you might confuse the enquirer by offering too many options. So it's worth considering asking a succession of forced-choice questions instead, moving from the general to the particular.

Leading questions

These lead the enquirer in the direction of the answer you want. You should only use them when you're 99% certain you do know what the enquirer wants. They can be dangerous, because they impose your assumptions on the enquirer's request, when what you really need to be sure of is that you haven't made any false assumptions. With type 1 (the homophone victim), you might ask, 'So it's *statistics* on their movements that you're looking for then?' Your enquirer might answer 'Yes', and be quite right. But you still don't know whether it's 'whales' or 'Wales'.

Hypothetical questions

These attempt to glean further information by putting a hypothetical situation to the enquirer. As with the multiple questions, you have to be able to think on your feet to come up quickly with a sensible hypothetical question. But they might be your only hope with type 6 (the muddler). This is because there is one hypothetical technique that allows you to ask the forbidden question: 'What do you *really* want?' Put this way, it sounds aggressive and suspicious and sends out the wrong signals to the enquirer. But it is frequently the question you really do need to ask. So you can put the same question in a hypothetical form by asking 'What would your ideal answer look like?' (Whether or not you ask a hypothetical question of your enquirer, this is one absolutely vital hypothetical question that you must ask yourself. We'll come back to it in Chapter 3.)

Agreeing the task

Whichever questioning technique you employ, the aim is the same. It's to find out, beyond any doubt, exactly what your enquirer wants you to do for them. For this you must be in full possession of the facts. Your chosen questioning strategy should allow you to do one or both of two things – funnelling and probing.

Funnelling focuses the enquirer in from the general to the particular. It would probably help with types 4 (the generalist) and 6 (the muddler). However it can also be an efficient way of dealing with the ambiguities offered by types 1 (the homophone victim), and 5 (the know-all). It's usually the easier of the two techniques to apply because it needn't sound over inquisitive or threatening. Closed, forced choice and leading questions are all suitable for funnelling operations – although you should bear in mind that each of these techniques carries its own hazards. Forced choice is almost always the most efficient one.

Probing seeks further details from the enquirer when you're not at all clear what they want; you would use the technique to try to find out the context in which the enquirer was thinking. It might help you with types 2 (the Chinese whisperer) or 4 (the generalist), and you'll certainly need to deploy this technique with type 7 (the obsessively secretive). But you have to exercise caution and tact when using it, because it can sound inquisitorial. Open, multiple and hypothetical questions might all help you to probe. On the whole, multiple questions are probably best here – they don't sound so inquisitorial, they show that you're trying to help and taking the enquiry seriously, and they're more likely to put the enquirer at their ease than on their guard.

Who, what, when, where, why, how?

'I keep six honest serving men – they taught me all I knew,' said Rudyard Kipling in the *Just So* stories. To answer any enquiry effectively, you need them too; they are the six questions: Who? What? When? Where? Why? How? Your enquirer will fill in some of the blanks relatively unprompted – once you've discovered what they really want, of course, as opposed to what they began by asking. Your supplementary questioning should either fill in or eliminate the others. The first four – Who? What? When? Where? – should provide essential information to enable you to answer the enquiry. The last two – Why? How? – could provide supplementary details that enable you to understand the subject of the enquiry, or the reason the enquirer wants the information, better. You should try to get answers to all six.

- Who? *means* Who are you interested in? (This could be a person, an animal, an organization, a civilization, a society, a movement.)
- What? *means* What are they doing that interests you?
- When? *means* Are we dealing with current, recent or historical information?
- Where? *means* Which localities, regions or countries do we have to consider?
- Why? *might mean* Why are they doing the thing you're interested in? *or could mean* Why are you, the enquirer, interested in this subject?
- How? *might mean* What methods are they using to do it? *or could mean* How do you, the enquirer, want the subject handled?

You wouldn't necessarily always take the questions in this order. (Kipling didn't.) Your enquirer's answers would fill in the blanks for some of them as you went along. Sometimes your questions will seek to elicit more information about the subject that the enquirer is interested in, and at other times you will be looking for information on why the enquirer is interested and how they want the subject handled.

Let's see how it might work for the questions to which our enquirers really wanted answers.

Type 1: The homophone victim
I'm looking for information on migration patterns in whales

So we need something like a big animal encyclopaedia then? (**Who** are we looking for?)
Oh, sorry – you mean people in Wales moving around? (**What** are they doing?)

Do you mean things like how they travel to work, or what they do when they move house? (**How** are they doing it?)

Is it just movements within the country, or from outside as well? (**Where** do we have to consider?)

Are you looking just for movements now – or back over a period? (**When** do we have to consider?)

Are you looking for information on why people move – or just the figures? (**Why** do you need the information?)

I'm looking for information on migration patterns in Wales

Verdict: Once you've got over the initial misunderstanding, you should be able to get all the way with this enquiry – it's precise and specific.

Type 2: The Chinese whisperer

I'm trying to find a song called When I would sing under the ocean

Right; have you any idea who sings it, or who it's written by? (**Who** are we looking for?)

I'm afraid I can't find a song of that title. How did you come to hear of it? (**How** can we take this enquiry forward?)

Oh, you heard it on the radio. Can you remember which station or programme? (**Where** did you hear it?)

Was it a pop song or something more traditional? (**When** might it have been written?)

Oh, so it was a baritone solo and you think it might have come from an opera or musical. (**What** kind of song was it?)

Since it's not showing up in any of our musical sources, perhaps the title's slightly different. Let's think of some other way of identifying it. (**Why** aren't we finding it, when the enquiry seems so straightforward?)

I'm trying to find a song called When I would sing under the ocean [*but the title is probably wrong*]

Verdict: At this stage in your questioning, you're not going to find out what you're really supposed to be looking for because the enquirer has got the question wrong. As far as you're concerned, you're still looking for a song called *When I would sing under the ocean* but just not finding it anywhere. However, several things that emerged during your questioning should help you to understand the challenges you face – particularly the fact that the enquirer discovered the title aurally. This should arouse your 'Chinese whisper' suspicions. Meanwhile you now have lots of ideas for places to try: the radio station that played the song, guides to opera and musicals, even asking the enquirer to hum the tune so you can look it up in a dictionary of musical themes or on a music finder website.

Type 3: The malapropist

Do you have the Electrical Register?

I'm sorry, I can't find a directory of that title. Is it electricians you're looking for? (**Who** are you looking for?)
Oh, I beg your pardon, I must have misheard – it's the voters' list you need. The local one? (**Where** are you interested in?)
And I presume you want the current one? (**When** do you want to cover?)
Are you just looking up a specific address, or do you need to browse through? (**What** kind of information do you need to find?)
So you're looking for people with particular surnames. Is this because you're trying to trace someone? (**Why** do you need the information?)
There might be other kinds of source we could use as well – online directories, for instance. What form would you like the information in? (**How** do you want the enquiry handled?)

Do you have the electoral register?

Verdict: In this instance, we've probably taken the line of questioning much further than is necessary to answer the enquiry – but it does go to show just how much may lie behind even the most apparently simple request. At the very least you will need to confirm that it is the current register for your local area that the enquirer wants; you shouldn't just assume that it is. And, of course, once you've realized the enquirer's initial mistake, you will need to respond tactfully so as to spare them any embarrassment.

Type 4: The generalist

Do you have any books on retailing?

Yes, plenty – and other kinds of information source as well. Are you interested in retail management, shop design or location, market research, special types of retailer such as food or electrical goods shops – or even one particular retailer?' (**Who** are you interested in?)

Ah, so it's Marks & Spencer; are you looking for financial information or news on the company's activities? (**What** do you need to know about them?)

So you need the latest accounts? (**When** are you interested in?)

Just its UK operation, or worldwide? (**Where** do we need to consider?)

Is it detailed information for investment purposes, or just a brief financial profile for information? (**Why** do you need the information?)

Do you need the figures in manipulable form? Downloadable onto a spreadsheet, for instance? (**How** do you want the information presented?)

What is Marks & Spencer's current pretax profit?

Verdict: This may be an over-optimistic scenario. Enquirers can be extraordinarily secretive about money matters, and here we reached the crucial company name remarkably fast. After that, however, the thing to bear in mind is that there is an enormous amount of business information available and it's easy to bury an enquirer under a deluge of semi-relevant information. So it's worth probing to find out precisely what they want.

Type 5: The know-all

Where do you keep the New Scientist?

The current issue is on the display racks, but we have back issues as well if you're looking for something specific? (**What** are you looking for?)

So you'd like to check some back issues of the journal as well. How far back would you like to go? (**When** do you think the article appeared?)

Are you looking for a particular article that you know appeared in the *New Scientist* or are you just looking for information on a particular topic? (**Why** do you need the *New Scientist* specifically?)

So it's information on radiation risks. If you can't spot the article you remembered from the *New Scientist*, would you like to check elsewhere as well? (**How** do you want to progress your enquiry?)

Probably the most efficient way to find further information on this topic would be to search online for references to articles that might have appeared in other scientific titles that we take. For example, *Nature* covers the same sort of subjects as *New Scientist*, and we have back files of that as well. (**Where** else would you like to search?)

I think I saw an article recently about the research that's been done into the health effects of radiation, both from artificial and natural sources, and who's doing it. I don't want to appear ignorant so I'm just going to ask for the latest New Scientist, *which is where I think I saw it. [In fact, the article appeared in* Nature, *and was published months ago.]*

Verdict: This may seem like going to enormous lengths to deal with what appears initially to be a very straightforward query. But it turned out not to be straightforward, and your tactful probing may have prevented the enquirer from leaving in a disgruntled mood after failing to find the article in the current *New Scientist*.

Type 6: The muddler

Have you got any books on Kew Gardens? That's to say, something on the Crystal Palace, if you can manage it. What would be really helpful, actually, would be the index to the Illustrated London News. *Or, better still, a book on tropical fish.*

That's a wide range of topics; is there a common factor? (**Who** (or what subject) are you interested in?)

So it's information on zoos; would it actually be aquariums? (**What** kind of zoos?)

Victorian ones? (**When** would this be?)

And is it particularly London you're interested in? (**Where** are these aquariums?)

Are you trying to do a general history of aquariums? (**Why** do you want the information?)

So you want to concentrate on one aquarium; which one would that be? (**How** do you want the enquiry to proceed?)

I'm doing a project on the Westminster Aquarium.

Verdict: Like type 4, this is probably an over-optimistic scenario. The true muddler would probably go on muddling for some time before giving you the opportunity to start funnelling. But one advantage that muddlers offer over generalists or the obsessively secretive is that they do at least give you plenty of clues.

Type 7: The obsessively secretive

Where's the catalogue?

We have an online catalogue but it only covers the books; can I help further? (**How** can I help you?)

So it's something in the newspapers? (**What** sort of information do you need?)

Do you know roughly when? (**When** should we start looking?)

Can I show you one or two websites that might help? What subject are you interested in? (**What** kind of information do you need?)

So it's the cash-for-questions affair – how would you like me to narrow the search down after that? (**How** would you like the enquiry to proceed?)

Ah, if it's a particular organization you want, a directory might actually help you better, or the organization might even have a website. (**Who** are you looking for?)

So you actually want something on how it's funded? Well, if it doesn't seem to have a website, let's see if we can find an article on it. (**What** is being done to this organization?)

Is it the race relations aspect you're interested in? For any particular purpose? (**Why** do you need the information?)

So it's school governorships? Sorry, I don't understand the connection with the cash for questions issue. (**Why** do you need to know this?)

It's a family connection? So it's a question of possible conflict of interest? (**How** are the two issues linked?)

So we're looking for something like the rules for school governors? (**How** do you want the subject handled?)

Cash for Parliamentary questions... Strong & Moral Britain Association... neo-fascist organizations... funding... school governors... declarations of interest.

Verdict: Like type 6, this is a somewhat compressed scenario. It would probably take a lot of very tactful questioning to elicit all the aspects of this complex and sensitive affair. Restricting your questioning to sources, delivery media and techniques, as opposed to the specific information required, will probably reassure your enquirer. Then you can use your demonstration of how the source or delivery medium works to find out more about what your enquirer actually wants.

Keeping good records

As you can see from these examples, some of your questions come out as requests for further information, others as reactions to information received. That's how it usually happens in real life; the responses to either type will help you to fill in more of the blanks. If it's an oral enquiry, or you can respond quickly by e-mail, now is the time to repeat back to your enquirer what you think they want you to do. Which brings us to the question of record-keeping.

Many libraries and information services use enquiry forms, and these can be laid out in innumerable different ways. They may be printed or electronic, and they may even form part of a sophisticated enquiry management system, where every enquiry is tracked right through to completion. There's an example of an enquiry form on pages xiv–xvii, designed especially for the techniques suggested in this book. Enquiry forms can allow you not only to record the enquiry, but also to list the sources checked and the time taken, collect valuable performance data on the degree of success achieved, and alert your organization to any new information or sources that might be useful to your colleagues in the future. (We'll take a detailed look at this aspect of record keeping in Chapter 9.) For the moment, though, you'll be using the form to ensure that you really do understand what your enquirer wants. Something like . . .

- *So we're looking for figures on how people have moved into, out of and within Wales between the 1991 and 2001 Censuses?*
- *So we're looking for a song that's a baritone solo that you probably heard on BBC Radio 2 last Sunday, with a title something like* When I would sing under the ocean?
- *So we need to browse through the current electoral register for this area?*

- *So we just need a single figure – Marks & Spencer's latest pretax profit?*
- *So we're looking for information on who's doing research into the health risks of artificial and natural radiation, and it's worth searching elsewhere if we don't find the article you remember from New Scientist?*
- *So we're looking for anything we can find on the Westminster Aquarium, which was demolished some time in the late nineteenth or early twentieth century?*
- *So we need: something on the funding of the Strong & Moral Britain Association; information on whatever rules affect school governors; and it would help to have something from the papers on the cash-for-questions affair?*

Note the use of the word 'we'. This is your problem now, as well as your enquirer's, and it is only good customer relations to make that clear by involving yourself in it.

Finding out how long you've got

Finally, you have to agree a deadline. Often, this will be 'now'. The enquirer will be standing there, and they'll want you to point them in the right direction straight away. (We'll deal with techniques for thinking on your feet in Chapter 3.) But, if the enquiry has come in by phone, e-mail, fax or letter, you need to be quite clear when the answer is required by. So don't take 'As soon as possible' or 'It's urgent' for an answer. 'As soon as possible' could mean next year, from your point of view, and urgency can be measured in minutes or days. So politely pin your enquirer down to a date and/or time. And if you think the timescale is unrealistically short, don't say 'Can't be done' – keep it positive. Explain that you will only be able to provide a limited answer in that time, and invite your enquirer to extend the deadline. More often than not, you'll find that they are able to give you more time. (We'll deal with meeting deadlines in Chapter 6.)

Coming next – not too little, not too much...

You now have nearly all the information you need to tackle the enquiry. But you still have to find out just one more thing – how much information your enquirer wants, and in what detail. Until comparatively recently, information on many topics was a scarce commodity. But increasingly now we're facing information overload, so whereas in the past it may simply have been a question of giving your enquirer whatever you could find, now you must have the courage to select and reject.

Information overload is such an important topic that we're going to devote an entire chapter to it. So in Chapter 2, we'll look at how to provide the right amount of information – not too little, not too much.

To recap . . .

- **Beware of the pitfalls presented by homophone victims, Chinese whisperers, malapropists, generalists, know-alls, muddlers and the obsessively secretive.**
- **Employ open, closed, forced choice, multiple, leading or hypothetical questions, as appropriate.**
- **Look for answers to the questions Who? What? When? Where? Why? How?**
- **Don't accept a vague deadline.**

CHAPTER 2

Not too much, now

Too much information is as bad as too little

> **In this chapter you'll find out how to:**
>
> - **recognize the dangers of overload**
> - **discover how much information your enquirer needs**
> - **work out the level of specialism**
> - **begin earmarking and eliminating potential sources and delivery media.**

There was once a little girl who was given a book to read as a homework project. At the end she had to write a report saying what she thought of it. So she did. She wrote 'This book tells me more than I wanted to know about penguins.'

Bear those penguins in mind as we move to the next stage of successful enquiry answering. First of all, remember a key lesson from Chapter 1 – are they Antarctic sea birds, paperback books or chocolate biscuits? But what really matters, here, is the lesson about 'more than I wanted to know'. If you think that finding information is hard, then rejecting it is even harder. It takes a lot of confidence to say to yourself, 'Now I've found it I realize I don't need it even though it's relevant.' There is always the nagging fear that you might be rejecting the one piece of information that your enquirer would have leapt at as the answer to all their problems. Of course, this shouldn't happen if you've done your questioning properly because, as well as discovering exactly what information they need, you should also have discovered how much, and at what level.

A decade or so ago, this wasn't an issue. In many cases, you found whatever there was to find in the one or two printed sources available to you, handed them over, and the enquirer probably then had the job of modifying their demands in the light of whatever you had been able to come up with. But the internet has changed all that. All of a sudden we've gone from a situation where information was a scarce resource, to be husbanded and cropped carefully, to a glut, in which it grows and reproduces unchecked – through discussion lists, blogs, wikis, etc. – and threatens to overwhelm us in an impenetrable jungle. There's a phrase for this: information overload.

Information overload

Twenty years ago, if you wanted to find a piece of information that you thought had been in the newspapers, there was really only one place you could go – *The Times Index*. Assuming that you were able to negotiate the somewhat eccentric indexing of our great newspaper of record successfully, you then had the option of actually looking up the story in *The Times* (probably on microfilm, a severe delaying factor in itself) or taking the dates as a basis and scanning through other newspapers for coverage of the same story. *The Times Index* came out several times a year – very late – and cumulated only into comparatively short periods, so unless you had a pretty clear idea of the dates you needed, you could easily consume the whole time allotted to your enquiry using this one retrieval tool only – and still fail to find the information.

There were some alternative sources you could try. The indexing of *Keesing's Contemporary Archives* (now *Keesing's Record of World Events*) was somewhat more efficient, and it cumulated more quickly. But *Keesing's* is an international source, containing far less information than a run of newspapers covering the same period. So if the story you were looking for covered a United Kingdom issue of comparatively little international importance, then *Keesing's* probably wouldn't help. You could also have tried *British Humanities Index* or what was then called *British Technology Index* (now *Abstracts in New Technologies and Engineering*) if you thought the issue might have been the subject of comment in contemporary journals. But both of these sources were highly selective in their coverage of the titles they indexed. By and large, therefore, your chances of failing to find the story or article you wanted were pretty high.

Much the same applied with books. You might find an entry for the book you wanted in the *British National Bibliography* or *British Books in Print*. You might even be able to borrow the book in due course, using the inter-library loan scheme. All the same, the number of places you could look for books was pretty limited, and if your book was out of print, or foreign, your chances of tracking it down were frequently slim.

Multiple media

Now just think how all that has changed. If you're searching for information in the newspapers now, you'll be using the web, not a printed index. Virtually all newspapers have their own websites, generally offering a selection of current stories free of charge and charging for access to a fully searchable archive as well. Rolls-Royce database services, such as Dialog or LexisNexis, will allow you to do precise, complex searches on newspapers, wire services and articles from business, technical and professional journals for years back.

It's just the same if you want to track down a book – whether it's in print or not. Not only do you have a whole armoury of online bibliographic services to try – including online bookshops such as Amazon.com – but you can even expect to see the complete texts of more and more out-of-copyright books coming available online through initiatives such as the Google Books Library Project.

The world wide web offers access to an almost unstoppable slurry of information, good and useless. This can sometimes lead people to think that they don't need library and information professionals any more; search engines like Google will find it all, they believe. It's certainly true to say that, whereas a few years ago you'd be lucky to find *anything* on most subjects, you now have the potential chance of finding *everything*. But 'everything' is almost certainly too much – and that's where you come in.

How much does your enquirer need?

So the last stage in your questioning is to find out more or less how much information your enquirer needs, and of what kind. In the past, 'Whatever you can find' was often the only realistic option. Now it's increasingly the *least* realistic one. You have the tools to bombard your enquirers with information, but you're not helping them if you do that, because they're looking to you not only to find the information they need but also to filter it, so that they end up with just enough to do whatever they want to do – no more, no less. To help them achieve this, you need to employ the same questioning techniques that we discussed in Chapter 1, and several question types will do.

You could simply ask an open question – 'How much information do you need?' But you might not get a very precise answer – 'Whatever you can find' doesn't really help you very much. Also some enquirers might feel daunted by the task of trying to imagine for themselves what the final answer might look like. That's your job – and we're going to return to it in some detail in Chapter 3. So a multiple question might be better – something like: 'Do you just want a few main points in note form, or a page or so of information, or something like an article, or a complete book?' This of course assumes that you have a fair idea of the form in which the information is likely to appear. But if it's a highly technical subject, or the enquirer has used terminology that is unfamiliar to you, you might not know what to expect. So a third possibility might be to put the hypothetical question: 'What would your ideal answer look like?' This again puts the onus back on the enquirer, so it's to be avoided if at all possible. But it may be your only hope if your enquirer has really taken you into totally unfamiliar territory. (Whether or not you ask the *enquirer* this question, it's an absolutely crucial one that you need to ask *yourself* – as we shall see in Chapter 3.)

Whatever the enquirer answers – and, in this case, the multiple question is likely to elicit the most helpful answer, from your point of view – you should now have a clear idea of the kinds of sources to go to first – and the best medium through which to access those sources. It may seem obvious, but it is vitally important to go to the best source first, using the most appropriate delivery medium – print, portable database, free web or paid-for online service. (We'll deal with sources and delivery media in the next couple of chapters.) If your chosen source, delivered through your chosen medium, gives you the answer you want then you can, quite simply, stop looking. It doesn't matter if there's more information to be found elsewhere; once you have found enough to satisfy your enquirer's needs you should stop. This isn't being lazy – it's practical.

Information for a purpose

Firstly, once you've found enough to meet one enquirer's needs, you can move on to the next one. That way, no-one is kept waiting longer than they have to be. Secondly, people rarely want information merely to satisfy their curiosity – they almost always need it for a purpose. Let's think about two of the commonest – school or college projects, and retirement hobbies.

However much you may privately regret a student's lack of curiosity, or deplore the narrow focus of a curriculum that forces this attitude upon them, you have to be realistic about it. You're not helping the hapless student or school child at all if you don't take a pragmatic approach. The fact is that they need enough information to allow them to get a good mark, and once they've got that, they can't afford the time to go browsing for more information because they've probably got three or four more projects or homework assignments coming up to deadline too. So help them to find what they want, and then when they've got enough – stop.

Retirement hobbyists, on the other hand, may be operating at the opposite extreme. They're delighted with every additional snippet of detail you can provide – even if they've read it in half a dozen other sources already. The danger here, of course, is that – in the nicest possible way – they can be terrible time-wasters. Whether you actually get carried along by their enthusiasm, or simply can't shake them off, you have to be systematic about your choice of sources to help them too – and the order of priority in which you use them. In both these cases, the aim is to help your enquirer become self-sufficient as rapidly as possible – to give them something to read, and get them settled down reading it.

Do-it-yourself?

Finally, you have to know just how much help to give. Teachers and lecturers are notorious at handing out projects with no thought whatsoever for the ease or difficulty of the research involved. You can easily be faced by two children from the same school class, one of whom wants to do a project on dinosaurs and the other on fourteenth-century Byzantine art, where the teacher appears to have given no thought whatever to the possibility that these might not represent tasks of equal difficulty. In these circumstances, you clearly need to get the dinosaur child started quickly, and devote the bulk of your attention to the Byzantine one. The same problems can apply to retirement hobbies, where people have the habit of devoting their declining years to researching the most esoteric topics (frequently family histories) about which the available information is spread very thinly indeed. Either way, the moral for you is clear: you must be able to work out, quickly, what are the most appropriate sources for the job and what is the best delivery medium to employ.

Working out the level of specialism

Exactly the same principles apply in working out the level of specialism your enquirer needs. You need both to probe and funnel to find out whether they are looking for information at postgraduate level or are starting from a position of total ignorance. You can use the same sort of questioning strategy as you did above when finding out the level of detail required, but you also have to be both tactful and suspicious. No-one wants to be thought ignorant, and it's only human nature for people to pretend to greater knowledge than they actually have. So you must use the answers to your Who? What? When? Where? Why? How? questions to judge how much your enquirer knows already. Again, this determines the types of source you use – a layperson asking about varicose veins wants *Black's Medical Dictionary*, but a student doctor probably wants articles from *The Lancet*.

There are different *types* as well as *levels* of specialism. An academic and a practitioner might be equally well qualified in their subject. But the academic, about to embark on a piece of original and mould-breaking research, may genuinely need to be aware of everything that has been written about a subject. A practitioner, on the other hand, whose job is to seek a solution to a practical problem, might be perfectly satisfied with just enough information to offer a good spread of options for taking a decision, for making a recommendation or for taking action. An enquirer who asks you for *Gray's Anatomy* may be a paramedic studying fractures; but may equally be an art student studying life drawing. So it is up to you to use your crucial questioning techniques to determine exactly the *quantity* and *quality* of information your enquirer needs.

Earmarking and eliminating potential sources and delivery media

We've actually mentioned a few specific sources in this chapter – *The Times Index*, LexisNexis, *Black's Medical Dictionary*. We've also briefly considered the different delivery media through which these sources may be available: print, online, CD-ROM. In reality, though, we haven't reached the sources and media stage yet. All we've done so far is to discover the subject required, how much information our enquirer wants, and at what level of detail. You may not have a clue yet what actual sources exist to provide the answer you want, or the delivery media through which they are available. But by now you should be able to start forming a judgment on the *kind* of source that will be most helpful, and the *most appropriate* delivery medium through which to access it. Equally if not more important, you can now start eliminating sources and media that are less likely to be useful. Remember – it doesn't matter if these less helpful sources and media have some of the information you need. Information overload keeps becoming more of a problem – not less. So you must have the courage to reject information – something which, it has to be said, library and information professionals have not always found easy to do in the past.

Coming next – avoiding panic, thinking on your feet . . .

Now at last you have all the information you need to actually start hunting for the answer. But where exactly? It's all very well imagining your ideal source, but how do you discover whether such a source exists and in what delivery media it can be made available? And how do you decide what to do first? In Chapter 3, we'll look at techniques for getting started on answering your enquiry.

To recap . . .

- ■ **Beware of information overload, and be ready to reject both sources and delivery media, and information.**
- ■ **Make sure you find out how much information your enquirer needs for the purposes of their task – too much is as unhelpful as too little.**
- ■ **Find out by tactful questioning what level of specialism is appropriate to your enquirer's needs, bearing in mind that academics and practitioners may have different needs.**
- ■ **Identify the most appropriate types of source and delivery media for the job, and concentrate on those first.**

CHAPTER 3

Getting started

Imagining what the final answer will look like

> **In this chapter you'll find out how to:**
>
> ■ **imagine what the final answer will look like**
> ■ **decide what kinds of source will provide that answer**
> ■ **start identifying actual sources.**

Let's go back again to your exams. Do you remember how alarming they could be? You'd turn the paper over, look at the questions and struggle to fight down the mounting waves of panic as you realized that you couldn't answer any of them. Within a few seconds, though, you'd start seeing through the actual wording to the topic behind it. 'Oh yes,' you'd say to yourself with relief, 'That's really a question about the Scottish succession, and this one's really about the League of Nations; I can do those.' Well, exactly the same thing can happen with enquiry answering. You've listened carefully to your enquirer. You've asked sensible questions. You know exactly what they want. Now your enquirer is waiting for you to help. And you haven't a clue where to start looking.

Fortunately, there are techniques for dealing with this. All you need is a few seconds' thinking time. You can buy this time with a positive response – something like: 'I'm sure I can help; let me just think for a moment where would be the best place to start.' But do you know you can really help? The answer is: yes, always. You may not be able to find the exact answer your enquirer wants. But you can always help.

What is the final answer going to look like?

So what do you actually do with the thinking time you've just bought? There's a fundamental technique of enquiry answering that you probably need to deploy with every enquiry you ever tackle. Remember that we said in Chapter 1 that there was one hypothetical question that you always had to ask yourself? Well this is where it comes in – and the question is:

What is the final answer going to look like?

What you should try to do to get started on any enquiry is to conjure up a picture in your mind's eye of what the final answer will look like. You can't yet see the fine detail, and you don't know yet whether there is a source that will provide that answer. But you do at least know how the answer will be laid out on the page or screen, and that's half the battle. Let's see how it would work with just some of the questions that our different types of enquirer posed in Chapter 1.

I'm looking for information on migration patterns in Wales
This is a request for information that will track and measure the movements of people. If it's about measurement then it will have to take the form of figures presented as statistics. However there could be textual commentary on the figures, and they could also be presented as a graph, chart or diagrammatic map.

I'm trying to find a song called When I would sing under the ocean *[but the title is probably wrong].*
At this stage, you don't yet know what you're really looking for. As far as you're concerned, the song title you're looking for is still *When I would sing under the ocean*. In theory, you should be able to find this in a list of song titles or, possibly, musical themes. Additional information you'd expect to find there would probably include the composer, lyricist, and maybe the longer work from which the song came – an opera or musical, perhaps. However, you already suspect that the enquirer has got the title wrong and you're looking for something that doesn't exist. So the final answer may have to take the form of advice from a musical expert.

What is Marks & Spencer's current pretax profit?
This is about as straightforward an answer to visualize as there can be – it's going to take the form of a single monetary figure, attached to a company name which you already know, with a very recent date. The figure may appear on paper, but because this is a business topic, and timeliness is important, you're more likely to find it on a screen.

I'm doing a project on the Westminster Aquarium
So we're looking for information on a Victorian building in London – not a first-rank one either, like the Crystal Palace (which our muddled enquirer mentioned). There'll be descriptive text and pictures but, because it's not a particularly important building, you're probably not going to find very much about it in any one place.

Cash for Parliamentary questions... Strong & Moral Britain Association... neo-fascist organizations... funding... school governors... declarations of interest
Quite a shopping list of different kinds of information here. If the cash for questions affair is a hot topic in current affairs right now, then this could take the form of fast-moving news, perhaps on a screen. For the Association, you need not only neutral information about its activities but (because it's dubious) also something probing and investigative. The school governor information is going to take the form of rules, regulations, codes of practice – that sort of thing.

These are by no means the only forms that final answers to enquiries could take. Other possibilities include technical diagrams, pictures, original historical records, bibliographies, recordings, multimedia presentations, not to mention information supplied by a real person. Once you have used your common sense and a bit of imagination to work out what the answer will look like, then you can start looking for actual sources, secure in the knowledge that you're going for the right kind.

What kinds of sources will do the job?

You're making good progress; you've eliminated a good proportion of your library or information service's resources because you know it's not going to help you with this enquiry. You're not thrashing round inefficiently, darting off in whatever direction serendipity takes you. You've remained clear headed and logical and you're well on the way to finding the right answer – even though you still don't know what actual sources exist to help you. So let's go back over these enquiries again, to decide what kinds of sources will provide the answer you now know you need.

I'm looking for migration patterns in Wales
You're looking for **statistics** on the movement of people. The **Census** is the principal source of statistics on people, so that's almost certainly the best place to start and, since there is lots of government statistical data available online, perhaps you can use the **web**. However, if the enquirer wants commentary on these migration patterns, or maps and diagrams, they might be worth looking for in a sociology or demographic **textbook** – or possibly in a **journal** produced by the Census-taking authority.

I'm trying to find a song called 'When I would sing under the ocean' *[but the title is probably wrong].*
In theory, some kind of **encyclopaedia**, **dictionary** or **database** of song titles would be ideal – and preferably one that's well indexed because of the common word at the start of the title. An alternative might be a **catalogue** of scores, sheet music or recordings. However, there's obviously something wrong with the question which is preventing any of these obvious sources from working. If some of the words are correct, then a good database of song titles, with an inbuilt search engine, may solve the problem by allowing random searching by keywords. Many radio station websites include **playlists**, so you could try this if you can pin your enquirer down to the actual station, date and approximate time. Thereafter, though, you may be thrown back on your own imagination and capacity for lateral thinking. If that doesn't work, you could seek help from a **specialist library**.

What is Marks & Spencer's current pretax profit?
All but the smallest of companies these days have a corporate **website**, so that's the obvious first place to look. Larger companies, like Marks & Spencer, also publish glossy **annual reports**, so that's an alternative. Failing that, something that gives information on a lot of companies – such as a company **directory** or **database**. Or perhaps you could use an index or database to search through the business pages of a **newspaper**, looking for news of the company's latest results.

I'm doing a project on the Westminster Aquarium
You're going to need a fairly specialist source – a detailed **textbook** on Victorian architecture, or a specialist **guide** to London's buildings. You're probably going to have to hunt through quite a lot of **indexes** to find anything at all. The whole thing has a distinctly nineteenth century feel to it, so

perhaps the enquirer's idea of the *Illustrated London News* is worth following up – if it's got a decent **index**. The building might even have 'friends' – enthusiasts who might share information about it on the **web**.

Cash for Parliamentary questions... Strong & Moral Britain Association... neofascist organizations... funding... school governors... declarations of interest
There's a lot here, so let's take the sources stage by stage.

For the cash-for-questions affair, you're going to need a really up-to-date news source – an **online** one seems the obvious solution. However 'cash-for-questions' is only one of many ways in which this issue could be described so, having used a **database** to establish the approximate dates where you should be looking, you may then have to scan through actual **newspapers** rather than relying on an embedded search engine to find the precise phrase. Alternatively, you could begin by scanning through **political weeklies** for an overview, and then go back to the **newspapers** for the appropriate weeks for the full detail.

Basic information on the Association might come from a **directory** or the Association's own **website**, but comment on its more dubious activities is more likely to have appeared as investigative journalism in **newspaper** features or **journal** articles. Because these may have appeared at any time in the past, you need a source that covers a lot of ground quickly – a printed journals **index** or search engine embedded in a news website would be cheap to use but could be either time-consuming or insufficiently precise. So you may need to resort to a charged-for **database** of articles.

The rules for school governors sound pretty specialist; some kind of **encyclopaedia** of education law might help, but maybe you'll have to refer your enquirer to a specialist education **information service** or **library** for this. However, common sense would suggest that there are bound to be **guidelines**, produced by the Government especially for school governors. They're probably free, and very likely available on the **web**. Alternatively you could try the relevant **government department** or even your own **local education authority**.

Identifying actual sources

So now at last we've reached the really hard part – trying to discover whether any actual sources exist that meet your ideal. This is the really daunting bit (isn't it?) – having to learn hundreds of sources and have their details always at your fingertips, so that you can be ready at all times to come out with an instant diagnosis that always seems so impressive when doctors do it. It's true – there are an awful lot of information sources available, and you can spend an entire career answering enquiries and still be discovering new ones on the day you retire.

But reassurance is to hand. First of all, successful enquiry work depends on constant daily practice, so the more you do it, the easier it becomes because you can remember more sources without ever having consciously learned them. (Actually this can be a danger as much as an advantage; if you get too used to going to one particular source, you tend to continue using it even if a newer, more efficient one becomes available.)

The other reassurance, though, is that you can function perfectly effectively by keeping just a few multi-purpose reference sources in mind. Take a look at the list on pages xviii–xx of this book – **twenty-five multi-purpose reference sources you can't afford to ignore**. Between them, they will get you started on a very high proportion of the enquiries you will encounter. They are only a start, of course, and many information professionals would dispute some of the choices and want to substitute alternative candidates of their own. Nevertheless, what these sources (or others like them) can do is set you on the track of other, more specialized sources that you can't possibly be expected to remember. So the basic principle is: to get to know a limited number of your most useful local sources – UK ones, in the case of the titles listed here – or the equivalent titles for your own country. If there's nothing published in your country that will do the job, bear in mind that there is probably an international equivalent – frequently (but not always) American.

Learning some basic sources

There's no great mystery to learning a good range of basic sources. If you're working in a public reference or educational library, it will already be well stocked with sources of this kind, and you can spend some time profitably in the early stages of your new job browsing through some of them to see what they can do for you. Two tips: concentrate first on the ones that are shelved behind the enquiry desk. They will be the ones that your more experienced colleagues have found the most useful over the years. And, secondly, when you are examining and evaluating an unfamiliar source, don't just flick through it at random, but make it do something for you. If it's a directory or a statistical journal, look up a specific organization or figure. If it's an encyclopaedia, follow up all the index references to a subject of your choice. If it's a database, give it a really complex task to perform and see how quickly it responds and how relevant its answers are.

Also behind the enquiry desk you may well find an information file, compiled by the staff – the fruit of years of accumulated collective experience of enquiry answering. Such files can be a goldmine of hard-to-find information, once tracked down never forgotten. It could be a simple card index, a database on your intranet, or a set of bookmarked favourite websites. Whatever form it takes, it will be well worth getting to know in detail, because it will be uniquely tailored to your own organization's information specialities and the kinds of questions your enquirers are in the habit of asking. (We'll return to FAQ files in Chapter 9.)

But what if you are operating on your own, with sole responsibility for the library or information service of a specialist organization and no-one to turn to for help? Then you should award yourself an afternoon off, go to your nearest large public reference library armed with the list of sources at the front of this book, and ask to see them. Then use them to find out which journals, directories, statistical serials, websites and databases will help you in your work. (We'll look at how to get started in a new job of this kind in Chapter 10.)

Coming next – focus, dynamism, complexity...

Once you've identified the best sources for your enquiry, you frequently have another decision to take: which delivery medium to use. Very many of the basic sources you use will be available in print, as e-books and as fully searchable databases. You may encounter the same information on the printed page, on a portable medium such as a CD-ROM or DVD, online via the web, or even delivered in a form suitable for a mobile device such as a Blackberry. Each medium raises different implications for timeliness, user-friendliness, flexibility, cost. So in Chapter 4, we'll think about the different media you could use, and the advantages and disadvantages that each offers.

To recap . . .

■ Remember that there are techniques you can learn for stopping your mind from going blank – without having to know any actual sources.

■ Begin by visualizing the final answer in your mind's eye – a long or short piece of continuous text, a list, table, diagram, picture, map, image on a screen.

■ Then think what kinds of source will provide this answer – textbooks, journals, statistical serials, directories, databases.

■ Finally, start looking for specific sources, bearing in mind that you will only ever have to learn a small number of multi-purpose reference sources in order to begin tackling most enquiries.

CHAPTER 4

More on choosing sources and media

How to decide which is the best delivery medium for the job

In this chapter you'll find out how to:

■ determine the focus, dynamism and complexity of any subject
■ compare the merits of printed sources, online services and portable databases
■ apply these principles to specific enquiries.

Here's a cautionary tale. Puzzled by why her teenage son was spending so much time on the computer when she knew that his first love was playing the guitar, his mother discovered that, every time he wanted to learn a new chord, he went online and downloaded the correct fingering from a guitar tutor website. Now, there are only a limited number of guitar chords and they don't change; so she took him along to the local music shop and bought him a book – indexed and thumb-tabbed – that showed the lot, with fingering diagrams. Result: he had a universal reference source for his chosen hobby and didn't have to waste his time surfing when all he really wanted to do was play. Moral: don't regard the web as a universal panacea; there are many kinds of enquiry for which it still isn't the best medium.

To judge from the media nowadays, you'd think that information retrieval had only just been invented, and that the only way to do it was online. Make no mistake – the internet is a vital tool of enquiry work, and the web is the best single enquiry answering tool we have. Screen-based media offer enormous advantages over print in allowing you to search rapidly through unimaginable quantities of content and providing instant access to your chosen information source.

But the fact is that ink on paper is still a uniquely valuable medium, and we should be very cautious about predicting its demise, because forecasts like that almost invariably come to grief. Screen-based media still don't match the flexibility you can achieve by spreading open publications out on a desk, marking their pages, arranging them in piles. By all means browse online for information and ideas; but when it comes to serious reading, print is a far more comfortable medium to use.

So, as well as deciding what the information your enquirer needs will look like, you also have to determine certain of its other characteristics before you can decide which medium to use.

Focus, dynamism, complexity

Faced with similar information available in a range of different media, you have to take decisions on which medium would be most appropriate for the job in hand. This involves deciding, for example, whether the information is fast-moving or hasn't changed for a long time, and whether it's about a single topic or is actually about how one issue impinges on another. Let's look at the various types of information you might encounter, and think about the types of source and medium best able provide it.

Focus: broad-based and comprehensive versus narrow and specific

We've already considered the dangers when an enquirer says 'Get me everything you've got on . . .'. It's very unlikely that they literally mean 'everything'. But sometimes people really do want a broad overview of a subject. They might be gathering background information as a preliminary to a more detailed study, or they may just be wanting to brief themselves for a meeting, interview or short-term project. For **broad-based, comprehensive** information, you could use:

- an entry in a general encyclopaedia (printed or electronic),
- a chapter in a textbook, or
- a complete textbook.

But if your enquirer has got beyond that stage, and is delving into a subject for more **narrow and specific** detail, you could try:

- an entry in a special encyclopaedia (printed or electronic),
- an index entry in a textbook,

- a report from a specialist organization (i.e. not a conventional publisher),
- a journal article (printed or electronic),
- a statistical table (printed or electronic),
- an entry in a directory (printed or electronic),
- a database record (in an online or portable medium), or
- a website or page.

Dynamism: static versus dynamic

Static information is complete – finished. It's a matter of history. That's not to say that new research won't be done into it in the future but, to qualify as static, the subject must have reached a full stop at the time your enquirer asks you about it. Deciding that information is static is a hazardous undertaking. Stonehenge may be thousands of years old, but *History Today* magazine might still have carried an article in its latest issue on new archaeological finds that tell us more about its purpose or method of construction. But, assuming that you are certain that the information you are being asked about really *is* static, the types of source you could use include:

- an encyclopaedia or dictionary (printed or electronic),
- a textbook,
- a selection of journal articles (printed or electronic),
- a statistical time series (printed or electronic),
- a directory (printed or electronic), or
- a database in a portable medium such as a CD-ROM.

With **dynamic information**, you can't rely on sources or media of the type shown above because you can't be certain that they will reflect the latest state of affairs. Nevertheless, there are degrees of dynamism; a weekly source may well be sufficient for keeping up to date with medical research, papers for which are frequently submitted months before publication. Stock market prices, on the other hand, can change second by second and require a real-time online database to keep up with them. Bearing in mind these variations, the kinds of sources and media you could use for dynamic information include:

- online news service (free or charged),
- online database (real-time or archival),

- teletext (broadcast screen-based current information),
- audiotex (constantly updated telephone recordings),
- press release,
- current newspaper,
- recent journal, or
- latest statistics.

One thing you may well find yourself having to do with dynamic information is **browsing** and **scanning**. There may just not be a sufficiently up-to-date index or searchable database for your purposes; or, if there is, you may not be able to afford to use it. So you might have no alternative but to read quickly through quite a lot of text – a selection of newspaper stories, perhaps, or a set of database records. (We'll look at rapid reading techniques in Chapter 5.)

Complexity: single-issue versus multi-faceted

Single-issue enquiries can almost always be summed up in a word or two or a short phrase – 'dogs' or 'town planning'. That doesn't necessarily mean, however, that information on them is going to be easy to find; you might be looking for rare occurrences of a single word or phrase buried in a mass of text. Nevertheless, for single-issue enquiries you might use:

- printed source (if easy to find),
- searchable database, either online or in a portable medium (if hard to find), or
- web search engine (if hard to find and no obvious specialist online source is available).

Multi-faceted subjects, on the other hand, are concerned with the impact of one issue upon another – something like 'the public health risks of rabies spreading from wolves to domestic dogs in central Europe' or 'the town planning law implications of non-retail uses of shops in conservation areas'. Fully searchable databases, with powerful search engines that permit the use of sophisticated search logic, are ideal for multi-faceted subjects. The strength of such database systems lies in their ability to make and break connections between disparate subjects almost instantaneously. Beware, however – not all databases can do this really effectively; web-based news services, for example, are built for speed of updating, not searchability, and web search engines don't usually allow you to build complex searches progressively, in the way you can with professional online services like Dialog or LexisNexis. (We'll look at efficient searching in Chapter 5.) So before you decide to use a database to answer a multi-faceted enquiry, make sure that it really *is* fully searchable. Having said that, your chosen delivery medium could be a:

- professional online service (especially if the multifaceted information is also dynamic), or (less likely) a . . .
- specialist database in a portable medium – e.g. on a CD-ROM (if the information required is multifaceted but also static), or a
- web search engine (if no obvious specialist searchable database is available).

Finally, a word of warning: the focus, dynamism and complexity of any subject will vary according to your perception of it. More often than not, this will depend on the environment in which you work. If you work in a specialist statistical or demographic library, for example, then you might regard the Welsh migration patterns query as pretty general, whereas someone in an all-purpose reference library would see it as very specific indeed. Also, there are two more types of information we need to consider in this context – information that is not available in-house, and information that is not in a published source at all. We'll return to these in Chapter 7.

Print, online and portable electronic media

The whole point about taking time to determine a subject's focus, dynamism and complexity is to help you decide which delivery medium would be most appropriate for the job. So before we try this out on some real enquiries, let's review the advantages and disadvantages of each.

- **Printed sources** are easy to handle, user-friendly and carry no running costs, so you can hand them over to an enquirer with the minimum of initial help. But they can also be out of date, slow to use if you are hunting for information buried in the text, and inflexible if their indexing doesn't accommodate the approach the enquirer wants to take.
- **Online services** (almost invariably delivered via a browser) can be right up-to-date, as well as being fast and flexible. But you'll need to take a decision on whether to go for a professionally edited commercial online

service, where accuracy and searching flexibility can be guaranteed but you have to pay for all the content you download, or for free websites, where you might be swamped with poor quality information.

- **Portable electronic media**, with their data stored on CD-ROM, DVD or even magnetic disk, can get you to the information you need fast and can permit sophisticated searching, usually with no running costs beyond the initial payment for the licence. But this medium is now completely out-classed by broadband online delivery via a browser. Because there is little incentive to invest in them, portable media often suffer from an old, user-unfriendly searching interface. Consequently, enquirers might be apprehensive about using them and want you to hold their hand. Added to this, their carrying capacity is limited, and they can still leave you with the nagging fear that, if you had opted to go online, you might have found much more. Plenty of cash-strapped information services have to continue using their old CD-ROM services to access archive material, so you may well come across this delivery medium from time to time, and have to get to grips with it. By and large, though, its use is diminishing fast.

The right medium for the job?

So how do these assessments work on the enquiries that our seven enquirers posed in Chapter 1? Let's quickly review them for their focus, dynamism and complexity.

I'm looking for information on migration patterns in Wales
Focus: Depends where you work and what sources you have access to; it's pretty broad-based if you have access to lots of statistical and demographic sources, but narrow and specific if you don't, because the enquirer wants one type of population data only.
Dynamism: Relatively static; censuses tend to be taken only once every ten years, albeit with more frequent intermediate population estimates.
Complexity: Fairly multi-faceted; although this is a standard census enquiry, it does involve combinations and permutations of people and places.
Verdict: Only one source will really do: the Census, since it's designed to answer precisely this kind of enquiry. Regarding delivery medium, the **printed** version may be sufficient, although the **online** version might allow even smaller movements to be identified.

I'm trying to find a song called When I would sing under the ocean *[but the title is probably wrong].*
Focus: Narrow and specific; only one answer will do, although the range of sources in which you might find it remains quite wide, as does the range of delivery media.
Dynamism: Static, presumably – unless it's a brand new song, of course. But if your enquirer is looking for a recording of it then you will need to use an up-to-date source to locate either a conventional recording that's in the catalogues, or a file-sharing service from which you can download it.
Complexity: Single-issue; one song, one composer, commonly requested information.
Verdict: A printed index of song titles should do in theory, unless the enquirer wants a recording – in which case you may have to use an online catalogue to identify one that's currently available. The problem is, though, that you can't find it anywhere. So perhaps there's something wrong with the question.

Do you have the electoral register?
Focus: Narrow and specific to the extent that only one source will do; but you still don't know whether the enquirer wants the local current register; they might need one of 10 years ago from the other end of the country.
Dynamism: Relatively static; electoral registers are revised once a year, but you need to beware of changes around the time the new one is due to appear – and you still don't know whether your enquirer wants the current local register or not.
Complexity: Single-issue, if your enquirer simply wants to check the names at a particular address; but if they want to use it for analytical or market research purposes, then the locally available printed version won't really help.
Verdict: Only one source will do, but as well as being locally available in **printed** form, it's republished **online** for various other purposes – usually as a high-cost credit checking and market research tool – and you need more information before you can hand it over with confidence.

What is Marks & Spencer's current pretax profit?
Focus: Narrow and specific, but the range of sources in which you could find this information remains wide.
Dynamism: Could be very dynamic; the announcement might only have come this morning, or might have been available for months.

Complexity: Single-issue; it's a common, readily available figure.

Verdict: Plenty of **printed** sources – financial directories, newspapers and journals – will give *an* answer, but almost none of them will be able to guarantee that it's the *latest* figure; if it really is only this single figure that's needed, then it seems pointless to look anywhere other than **online** via the company's **website**. (We'll look at getting the best out of the web in Chapter 5).

I'm looking for information on who's doing research into the health risks of artificial and natural radiation, and it's worth searching elsewhere if we don't find the article I remember from New Scientist

Focus: Narrow and specific; the enquiry is precisely defined, although not in the form in which our know-all originally expressed it.

Dynamism: Could be quite dynamic; even if the enquirer was wrong about the current issue of *New Scientist*, it's still pretty clear that research has been going on recently – and almost certainly back over many years as well.

Complexity: Multi-faceted; information on health risks alone won't do, and nor will information on radiation. The two concepts have to be considered together in the same document for the answer to be relevant.

Verdict: To find information on this one topic from among the mass of scientific content offered even by two titles like *New Scientist* and *Nature*, and to be sure it's up-to-date, it's going to be essential to use an **online** delivery medium. It's tempting just to use a generic web search engine, but a professionally edited archive **database** that can accommodate fairly complex search logic would be a much safer option. And if you do find references to articles in *New Scientist* and *Nature*, you can offer your enquirer the **print** versions to read; these will be much easier on the eye than trying to read from a screen, or even from a downloaded PDF printed out on your local printer.

I'm doing a project on the Westminster Aquarium

Focus: Pretty broad-based to the extent that anything you can find will be helpful, so there are lots of potential places you could look; once you start looking, however, you'll be looking for something very narrow and specific.

Dynamism: Static; this Victorian building was pulled down years ago, and was never of the first rank anyway.

Complexity: Single-issue, although information on it is going to be fairly thinly spread among a lot of sources.

Verdict: Not going to be easy to find; you'll have to skim rapidly through the indexes and contents pages of a lot of books. Your muddled enquirer might at least have inadvertently given you a lot of ingenious **printed** sources to try – books on Victorian architecture, fish displays, the *Illustrated London News*. However, since this is likely to be an obscure subject, it's certainly worth checking **online** – using a generic search engine, for once. (We'll look at search engines in Chapter 5).

Cash for Parliamentary questions... Strong & Moral Britain Association... neo-fascist organizations... funding... school governors... declarations of interest
Focus: Broad-based and comprehensive? Not really; it's actually a whole range of narrow and specific enquiries.

Dynamism: Pretty dynamic, although variably so; the cash-for-questions issue could be changing from day to day; with the Association it's difficult to say without checking – the possible neo-fascist connection could be a current issue or might not have been covered for years; rules on school governors are probably subject to fairly regular review to keep up with education policy.

Complexity: Multi-faceted throughout. The press might have handled the cash-for-questions affair in any number of different ways and probably only a searchable archive database will find them, although if it's very current and your enquirer is sure of the dates, you could scan through current newspapers and journals (using some of the rapid reading techniques outlined in Chapter 5) or use the archive section of a newspaper website. You might well need a searchable database, too, to establish any neo-fascist connections with the Association and to locate information on its funding. Finding general information on school governors' duties and obligations might be fairly straightforward, but what the enquirer has actually asked for is very specific information on declarations of interest.

Verdict: This difficult and sensitive enquiry will need a wide range of sources: searchable archive **databases**; **printed** news sources and directories; quite likely the **web** too; and probably discreet contact with **officials**. It's going to be time-consuming as well. (We'll look at deadlines in Chapter 6.)

By the way, did you notice something? Look back at the Focus category in these seven examples; they're nearly all 'narrow and specific'. That's how it should be by this stage, most of the time. Even if your enquirer originally asked a very broad question, and you decide ultimately to use broad-based sources such as general encyclopaedias or textbooks, your enquirer will usually have a more specific reason for asking. This should have come out during your question-and-answer session, and it is on this specific requirement that you must concentrate now.

Coming next – searching efficiently and quickly...

Now that we know exactly which sources we're going to use, and the most efficient delivery media for the purpose, we can actually get down to looking things up. In Chapter 5, we'll think about strategies for systematic and efficient searching.

To recap . . .

- **Distinguish between broad-based and narrow, static and dynamic, single-issue and multi-faceted enquiries.**
- **Remember the relative merits of printed sources, online services, whether current or archive, and portable electronic media.**
- **Bear in mind the types of medium best suited to the focus, dynamism and complexity of each enquiry**

CHAPTER 5

Do I really know what I'm looking for?

Tips for efficient search strategies

In this chapter you'll find out how to:

■ **decide what order to try the sources in**
■ **search systematically**
■ **change tack if necessary**
■ **get the best out of the web**
■ **employ rapid reading techniques.**

We've spent the last four chapters negotiating a labyrinthine and treacherous maze populated by enquirers who don't know or won't tell you what they want, can't speak the language or know too much for their own good. Faced with agonizing decisions on which turnings to take, we've drawn up a careful map of sources and delivery media that will stop us going round in circles, enable us to pick out the main route and skillfully avoid the dead ends. So are we finally out of the maze? No chance! We're right in the middle. To get out again, triumphantly bearing the answer, we've got to go through the whole process once more, in reverse.

Why? Because the pitfalls we will encounter while actually doing the searching are exactly the same as the ones we faced when trying to find out what our enquirers wanted in the first place. This time, however, we'll be pitted against indexes that lead you to the right word but the wrong subject, 'see' references that lead you nowhere, 'see also' references that take you on a circular tour, and databases that resolutely refuse to tell you anything at all. You don't believe it? Wait and see.

Where to search first

First of all, you have to decide which of the sources and delivery media you've identified as likely candidates to try first. Once again, this will depend on decisions you've already taken on the nature of the subject, the level of detail and specialism, and its currency and complexity. Possible options are:

- the most **up-to-date** source
- the one most **relevant** to the subject
- the one most **appropriate** to the task in hand.

Let's see how this might work in practice. We'll have a look again at some of our sample enquiries, for which we've now targeted likely sources.

I'm looking for information on migration patterns in Wales
You already know you're going to use the Census to answer this question. It wins on two of the three counts – it's **relevant** (all about population and their movements) and **appropriate** (you're looking for figures). It's as **up-to-date** as you'll get (2001) but it's also a vast document, with many specialist volumes. So you'll have to decide whether to go for the migration volume or the Wales volumes first. Alternatively, you'll need to consider whether the added flexibility and greater level of geographical detail that an electronic version might offer would justify the extra skill you'll need to deploy in using it. You'll also have to consider where to look for later estimates of population movements since 2001 (more **up-to-date** but less detailed), and whether you need to look for textbooks or journal articles for background commentary on the trends (just as relevant, perhaps more **up-to-date**, but possibly less **appropriate** because not primarily statistical).

I'm trying to find a song called When I would sing under the ocean *[but the title is probably wrong]*
Go for the most **relevant** source first – an encyclopaedia, dictionary or (authoritative) website that lists song titles. They don't necessarily have to be particularly **up-to-date** – unless your enquirer wants to buy a recording, in which case a current catalogue or website will be essential. Of course, all the evidence so far suggests that the title is wrong and that no amount of looking up, in print or electronic sources, is going to unearth it. So it may turn out that asking a musical expert is the most **appropriate** course of action.

What is Marks & Spencer's current pretax profit?
You should really go for an **up-to-date** source first if you can, since you clearly need to be sure you have the latest figure. The most obvious starting point would be to see if the company had a website (we'll look briefly at web searching later in this chapter). Failing that, you could try a company directory that gives financial details; it's a **relevant** and reasonably **appropriate** source, but being **up-to-date** is what really matters here.

I'm doing a project on the Westminster Aquarium
You're going to have to try to find **appropriate** sources here – illustrated books on Victorian architecture or guides to the buildings of London. Being **up-to-date** will be no help at all, and your chances of finding a **relevant** source (a book or article on the Westminster Aquarium itself) are virtually zero.

Cash for Parliamentary questions… Strong & Moral Britain Association… neo-fascist organizations… funding… school governors… declarations of interest
Very difficult to decide what to go for here. You probably need to be **up-to-date** for the cash-for-questions aspect, since the story may still be developing – so use an online news service or scan through the papers themselves. For the Association, a professionally edited archive database – or possibly a generic web search – seems the most **appropriate** starting point, since you will need to test speculations about funding and links with neo-fascist organizations. For the guidance for school governors, the school itself might seem the most **relevant** place to go, but it's hardly **appropriate** since your enquirer doesn't want to alert the school; the more remote Department for Education and Skills or the local education authority are equally **relevant**, and far more **appropriate**.

Searching systematically

Now you've finally decided on your first source and delivery medium, what are you going to search for? Plenty of things can go wrong, and you have to be ready for them. It's all really a matter of common sense, but you must spend a few moments thinking out your strategy. Among the myriad things that can cause problems, these are some that you should certainly consider:

Variant spellings

Whether you're using a conventional index or a database, variant spellings can cause big problems, so try to anticipate them. Proper names are especially tricky; it was Cain who killed Abel, but Kane who had a sled called *Rosebud*. And where on earth do you start looking for the fast food chain that calls itself *Mc*Donalds but calls its culinary *pièce de résistance* a Big *Mac*? Many of the databases, and quite a few of the printed sources, that you use will be American, so you will have to watch out for 'color' instead of 'colour', 'disk' instead of 'disc', 'skeptical' instead of 'sceptical'. This may not be a great problem with alphabetical indexes; your eye will quickly spot the difference. But, with many databases, you're flying blind, and if you search for 'favourite' or 'labour', an American database will keep on giving you a zero result no matter how much you swear at it. There are plenty of other pitfalls with variant spellings in British English – jails can be gaols, choirs can be quires (in more archaic sources anyway) – one could go on but that's enough.

Homonyms

If you're looking for hardware but keep coming up with foodstuffs then you've hit the homonym problem associated with 'nuts', which is equally at home in the two phrases 'nuts & bolts' and 'monkey nuts'. Numismatists studying the indented wax symbols at the base of legal documents run the risk that their hunt for 'seals' will lead them to sea mammals. And specialists in literacy keep finding themselves being vexingly directed to a large Berkshire town when they look up 'reading'. You need to be particularly alive to the dangers of homonyms, and be ready with tactics for taking evasive action if necessary. It's particularly – but not exclusively – a problem with free-text database searching (including on the web). Strategies that you can employ to deal with it include adding a further qualifying term to your search – such as 'numismatics' or 'literacy' – or, in the case of the 'nuts' problem, using a trade classification code (if one is available) instead of the word. In fact, whenever you use a searchable electronic source, do click on any buttons that look as if they might lead to an onboard thesaurus or other searching aid.

British versus American terminology

Many databases, and quite a few really good printed reference sources, are American, so it's important to be aware of American terminology. We all watch Hollywood movies (or do we mean films?), so most people would probably remember to use 'elevator' instead of 'lift', 'streetcar' instead of 'tram' and 'pants' instead of 'trousers' (although this last one presents its own special homonym problems as well). But how many Europeans know that the American for 'central heating' is 'space heating', and is equally unfindable whether you are using a database or a printed index?

Finally, remember that dates are cited differently in America and Europe; 9/11/2001 is September 11 in America but 9 November in Europe.

Synonymous, broader, narrower and related terms

Really well constructed indexes are based on a thesaurus which allows for all the different approaches that a searcher could take towards a subject. Alas, however, the real world is full of ineptly constructed indexes. 'Amateur' indexes, probably compiled by the book's author, may be full of elementary mistakes that a professional indexer would avoid. Such indexes might include an entry for 'railways', for example, but fail to add a parallel one or a reference for 'train services'. A professional indexer – a member of the Society of Indexers, for example – would avoid such mistakes; but a professional indexer will probably be on a fixed fee based on the estimated time taken to complete the job, so may not have the time to index down to the level of detail that would be helpful to you. So it's wise to assume that, whatever kind of index you encounter, it will have its limitations and there will come a point where you will have to fend for yourself.

Whether you're using a printed index or a free-text database, you're likely to have jotted down a list of possible words and phrases to search under before you start. That's fine as far as it goes, but with only a little extra effort, you can create a far more valuable searching aid for yourself. So instead of just jotting down those words and phrases randomly, in the order they occur to you, try listing them in a structured way. What you'll be doing is creating your own mini thesaurus, specially designed to help you with your current enquiry. It will minimize your chances of missing something relevant and – just as important – it will help you to avoid wasting your time by accidentally going over the same ground twice.

Let's see how this might work in practice. Suppose you've been asked for information about some aspect of railway management. You might start by randomly jotting down:

> **train services**
> **commuting**
> **public transport**
> **rail services**
> **surface transport**
> **fixed links**
> **rapid transit**

There are some pretty useful words and phrases here, including probably some that you wouldn't initially have thought of for yourself. So how do you think of suitable words and phrases in the first place? You could discuss the topic with colleagues, of course, and see what ideas they come up with. But a really good method when you're working alone is to start discussing the topic with yourself in your head – or even out loud, if that makes it any easier. Listen carefully to the words and phrases you are using when you do this, and note them down as they occur to you. That will give you the makings of an initial list of search terms.

But then you can add a lot more value to this list by rearranging these terms in some sort of hierarchy. Going back to look at that random list, you could start with:

> **rail services, train services**

These are your **root terms**, the basic words (or, in this case, phrases) under which you will usually start looking. For all practical purposes, they're synonymous terms, so you'll need to check under both, since they will be separated alphabetically in a printed index and, if you're using a search engine, typing in one of the phrases is unlikely to reveal information indexed under the other.

Then you need to think of some **broader terms**, for those occasions when you encounter an index (whether printed or electronic) that isn't as specific as this. These broader terms go above the root terms, at a different level of indentation to show their place in the hierarchy. So you might add:

> **public transport, surface transport, fixed links**
>   rail services, train services

Other indexes that you encounter might be much more detailed, and retrieve far too much information under your broader terms or even under your root terms to be useful. (Remember always to be alive to the dangers of information overload.) So you will also need to think of some more specific, **narrower terms** that meet your enquirer's precise requirements. Perhaps something like:

> public transport, surface transport, fixed links
>   rail services, train services
>   **commuting, rapid transit**

Once you've been through this little exercise, stick to it when searching and you'll be sure you're making the most efficient use of your time (but see 'Changing tack' below).

Changing tack ('see' and 'see also' references)

It's when things start to go wrong that your careful preparation for searching will really pay off. Hunting for information is a journey into the unknown. Every source you use will be differently constructed, and have its own indexing quirks. As your searching progresses, you're bound to come across relevant words and phrases that you never thought of in the first place, and that's when you'll have to take the difficult decision on whether it's worth going back over sources that you've looked at already.

If you do, your mini-thesaurus should at least help to ensure that you don't merely repeat work that you've already done. Let's go back to those train services; suppose you're onto your third or fourth possible source, and you suddenly find the following entries:

- Commuting *see* Suburban rail services
- Rapid transit *see also* Light rail

These entries show two further terms that you hadn't thought of before. The 'see' reference should mean that there are *no index entries at all* under 'commuting' (the term you first searched on), and that *all* the entries are under 'suburban rail services' (the indexer's preferred term). With the 'see also' reference, on the other hand, there could be relevant entries under *either* 'rapid transit' *or* 'light rail'. This is because, for the purposes of this index, they're similar but not identical, and the indexer created the 'see also' reference to be helpful.

These discoveries should prompt you to do two things. Firstly, you must amend your mini-thesaurus. There's no great problem with 'suburban rail services'; it's clearly at the same level of hierarchy as 'commuting'. 'Light rail' is a bit more tricky, though; it's not quite at the 'rapid transit' level, but then it's not quite at the 'rail services' level either. It's a related term, sitting somewhere in between. (It should also prompt you to continue the discussion in your head and come up with the additional term 'trams', which fits in more or less at the same level.) So your mini-thesaurus will now look something like this:

> public transport, surface transport, fixed links
>   rail services, train services
>   commuting, rapid transit, **suburban rail services**
> **(light rail, trams)**

The second thing you have to do is decide whether or not to go back over previous sources and recheck them for the new terms. This is where your systematic approach really pays off, because if you do decide to go back to previous sources, you can do so secure in the knowledge that you only have to check under the newly discovered terms, since you can guarantee that you've already searched systematically under the terms you thought of in the first place. If there's nothing extra to be found under the new terms, then you should be able to abandon the source without wasting any more time on it. (We'll discuss efficient management of your time in Chapter 6.)

Searching databases efficiently

Printed indexes will use 'see' and 'see also' references with varying degrees of efficiency and consistency. Databases, on the other hand, can offer a whole range of further searching aids. They may be able to display an alphabetical list of the words and phrases adjacent to the one you've chosen. They might be based on a structured thesaurus, which you can actually call up on screen and examine for possible further search terms. They may employ a hierarchical numeric classification (such as a trade classification) which will automatically retrieve all records classified below the point at which you actually enter. They'll almost certainly allow you to use truncation, so that a search on the term 'rail*' can automatically retrieve 'railway' and 'railroad' (and 'railings', so beware!).

Searching software will frequently return results ranked for relevance (treat this facility with caution, however; the software's idea of what's relevant frequently won't be yours or the enquirer's). Natural language searching, in which the software can actually interpret a phrase like 'Travelling in to work by train', is another possible facility; it can allow you to leave an enquirer searching for themselves while you attend to somebody else. (We'll deal with prioritizing enquiries to make the most efficient use of your time in Chapter 6).

Sometimes an 'advanced search' or 'power search' facility will offer you the option of using Boolean logic. Provided the database you are searching on has been efficiently indexed, this can be a very powerful retrieval tool indeed. Boolean logic works by linking words or phrases together using the logical operators OR, AND and NOT. It works like this:

A search on: apples OR pears   will retrieve every document that mentions apples *and* every document that mentions pears (including of course documents that mention both).

A search on: apples AND pears   will retrieve only documents that mention *both* apples *and* pears. Documents that mention *only* apples or *only* pears won't be retrieved.

A search on: apples NOT pears   will retrieve documents that mention apples, but *not* when they also mention pears (and will of course retrieve *no* documents at all that mention only pears).

There are refinements to Boolean logic, allowing you to specify that words must be adjacent to or within a certain number of words of each other. This lets you search for a phrase such as 'Land of Hope and Glory', ignoring the common (and usually non-retrievable) words in between the important ones. You can also usually bracket groups of words and phrases together, as in:

(apples AND pears) AND (farming OR horticulture) NOT (England OR Wales)

'Advanced search' or 'power search' facilities frequently hide this logic behind online searching forms. These may allow you to specify, for example, that you want to retrieve an *exact phrase*, or would be content to retrieve documents containing *any* of the words you specify, or only want documents that contain *all* of the words you enter. Such forms will also allow you to exclude words and phrases you specifically don't want to retrieve, and will probably also offer filters. These may allow you to limit your search by date, language, country, internet domain name – or even exclude 'adult' content. Whatever on-screen facilities you are offered for constructing your search, you can be sure that Boolean logic is behind it.

And lastly, whatever help is at your disposal with your database searching, you must still be ready to modify your searching strategy in the light of information retrieved – and to do so systematically.

Getting the best out of the web

Although it has its limitations, there's little doubt that the web is now the single most effective enquiry answering tool we have. There is an enormous quantity of high quality information available free on the web – from public bodies, from non-governmental organizations such as professional associations or charities, from academic sources and from international bodies. Reputable commercial sites frequently offer some free information as a taster to tempt you to buy more specialized charged-for services; there's nothing wrong with this, so make the best use you can of the information that is freely available, and take a decision on whether you think it's worth purchasing more.

The web is still not going to be the answer to everything, and is usually best used in combination with other professionally edited sources, which may themselves be print or electronic. Nevertheless, most of our seven enquiries would be worth a try on the web at some stage . . .

I'm looking for information on migration patterns in Wales
As more and more government information – particularly statistical data – is published on the web, it's an obvious port of call for this query.

I'm trying to find a song called When I would sing under the ocean *[but the title is probably wrong]*
The web offers plenty of file sharing services allowing users to download songs, so a few of these services would be an obvious initial port of call for

this query. Of course, since the song title is wrong, these visits would be unsuccessful – but this would very quickly tell you that you have a problem and that you will need to tackle the query in a different way. On the other hand, you may even find a site that has a 'sounds like' facility which could solve the mystery straight away.

Do you have the electoral register?

Of all these enquiries, this is the one for which the free web is perhaps the least suitable. Electoral register data is available online, but only for example through commercial credit checking agencies, which would require you to register first and would charge heavily for access thereafter.

What is Marks & Spencer's current pretax profit?

Almost all major institutions, and very many tiny ones, have promotional websites, so the web is particularly good at providing information on named organizations. It's therefore the obvious choice for the Marks & Spencer enquiry – especially as the information required is subject to regulation, so its accuracy on the Marks & Spencer site can be guaranteed.

I'm looking for information on who's doing research into the health risks of artificial and natural radiation, and it's worth searching elsewhere if we don't find the article I remember from New Scientist

Although the web might not necessarily yield many complete articles or scientific papers that you can rely on, you may well find bibliographic references to those articles, and perhaps be able to purchase the complete articles online from academic journal publishers. However, with the growth of the open access movement (see page 55) in academic circles, one can expect the number of authoritative professional and academic papers available freely on the web to grow rapidly. And the web could certainly help you identify some of the organizations that are active in this research field.

I'm doing a project on the Westminster Aquarium

The web is a great place for enthusiasts to pursue their individual obsessions, however esoteric – so a quick speculative search for material on the Westminster Aquarium might pay dividends.

Cash for Parliamentary questions... Strong & Moral Britain Association... neofascist organizations... funding... school governors... declarations of interest

Newspaper websites might get you started on the 'cash-for-questions' part of the query, although you need to bear in mind that the enquirer wants to link the issue to a named individual, so you may have to use the site's paid-for archive section and the 'advanced' or 'power' search option. The web is a natural home for pressure groups, so an anti-racist organization's site may well yield useful cautionary information about the Strong & Moral Britain Association – but you need to be sure you can trust the anti-racist organization, so check its credentials in a professionally edited source such as a directory first. And the wealth of public service information now freely available on the web means that you could well find guidelines for school governors.

As with all the other delivery media you use, do make sure that you are systematic in your web searching. Web pages are littered with tempting links to other sites, and if you are induced to follow any, make sure you don't forget what your enquirer's question was in the first place. Bear in mind, too, that there's little if any quality control over many websites, so there's no guarantee that what you find will be authoritative or accurate. So do satisfy yourself that the organization whose site you are using can be trusted; look it up in a reliable directory before committing yourself. After all, the enquirer will blame you – not the website – if you provide inaccurate or biased information.

Finding out what's worth having

So how on earth do you find out what's worth having on the web? Firstly, by using your common sense; if you've heard of the organization whose site you're visiting, and know it to be reputable, then obviously you can take the content of the site on trust. But how can you be sure that it is the organization you think it is? Sometimes internet domain names are not registered by the organization that you would expect to own them but by someone else – even occasionally for unscrupulous motives. So try firstly using a reputable printed or online directory to find details of organizations that are likely to help (including their web addresses), and then go from there directly to their websites. There's no shortage of sources that will help you find reputable websites; practically any professionally edited reference source will give you web addresses that you can follow up.

Meanwhile, though, the web continues to encourage some remarkable innovations in publishing, and they all offer both opportunities and challenges for the information professional. Let's consider three: blogs, wikis and the open access movement.

Blogs (short for 'weblogs') are online diaries that anyone can create and post on the web, using simple software. Their numbers are growing at an extraordinary rate and, by their very nature, they are completely uncontrolled. Some of the main search engines enable you to search blogs specifically. (We'll come to search engines in a moment.) You can find blogs on the most esoteric of subjects, offering not only information but also the possibility of putting your enquirer in touch with a blogger who may be able to help them directly with their query. Obviously if you recognize a blogger as an acknowledged specialist in their field – contributing a regular column to a trade or professional journal, for example – then you can presumably trust the blog. If you don't, then double check the blog's information elsewhere as well.

Wikis are websites that anyone with access to the internet can contribute to and edit simply by clicking on an 'edit this page' link. The best known is *Wikipedia* (www.wikipedia.org), a communal encyclopaedia. Conventional wisdom might suggest that wikis are inherently untrustworthy because anyone can amend them irrespective of their qualification to do so. However, they also tend to be self-correcting, as errors or omissions are spotted by others and amended accordingly. Entries on more recent topics may be somewhat unstable and require verification elsewhere. But entries on older topics may in some instances be fuller, more balanced and more up-to-date than entries in equivalent conventionally edited publications. So wikis are certainly worth considering as a fairly reliable information source.

Open access is a movement among academics, researchers and professionals to make the full texts of their articles and papers freely and permanently available online to anyone who wants to use them. There are two complementary forms of open access publishing. Either authors can provide access to their own published articles, by making their own electronic copies available free for all. Or journal publishers can provide free access to the articles – either by charging the author or institution for refereeing and publishing them (instead of charging the user for accessing them), or simply by making their online edition free for all. As the open access movement grows, it should result in more and more high quality peer-reviewed content, whose reliability you can trust, being made available on the web.

Searching with a purpose

Speculative searching probably means using search engines. These index the contents of the billions of web pages available and usually attempt to rank them for relevance. For most people, the term 'search engine' is now synonymous with Google (www.google.com). Google certainly is a remarkable phenomenon in terms of the relevance and scale of its retrieval capabilities. But no search engine is comprehensive in its coverage, and Google isn't the only one around. Some of the others include:

- AltaVista (www.altavista.com)
- Ask Jeeves (www.ask.com)
- Excite (www.excite.com)
- Go (http://go.com)
- Looksmart (http://search.looksmart.com)
- Lycos (www.lycos.com)
- MSN Search (http://search.msn.com)
- Yahoo! (www.yahoo.com)

In addition, there are several 'meta' search services, which search the other search engines. They obviously increase your chances of retrieving something if you're having problems finding anything, but they don't necessarily allow you to take advantage of the individual search engines' special characteristics. The best known ones are:

- Dogpile (www.dogpile.com)
- Mamma (www.mamma.com)
- Metacrawler (www.metacrawler.com)
- Webcrawler (www.webcrawler.com)

Search engines frequently have UK or other country equivalents, enabling you to limit your search to one country's sites. You'll be able to link to these from the main search engine site, or you could try experimenting by substituting .co.uk for .com at the end of the search engine web address. (In some cases, if you go to a search engine site from a UK web address, then you'll automatically be linked to the UK version of the search engine.) As we have already discussed, search engines frequently have 'advanced search' or 'power search' facilities, allowing you to use slightly more sophisticated search techniques, incorporating the Boolean logic that we discussed earlier, and hopefully allowing you to achieve more precise results.

On some search engine sites, the window where you type your search terms is surrounded – almost overwhelmed – by vivid and enticing links to other services: news, weather, travel, stock prices, horoscopes, lonely hearts, and much more. This can sometimes be useful, but it's just as likely to be a nuisance if you simply want to do your own searching with no off-putting diversions. Other search engines remain sparse and uncluttered, and this may be more to your liking. There's no particular reason why you should automatically stick with one search engine. So experiment with them all, ask your colleagues' opinions, and reach your own conclusions.

Even though they each index only a fraction of the web's total content, search engines do still tend to produce vast numbers of hits, and it's not always obvious why some items have been retrieved at all. Sometimes, links may even be given prominence on search engine results because sites have paid for them, so beware. Often, it's more efficient to start with a search engine, but then to follow links as soon as you get to a nearly relevant site. For example, you could try putting in a search that goes something like…

"school governors" (rules regulations guidelines) uk

… then pick the most promising result out of the first few (possibly the site of one particular local education authority or school) and follow links from there to the site of an authoritative national institution. However, as mentioned over and over again, a particularly effective way of using the web is in combination with other, professionally edited sources – so you might find an organization's web address in a directory or advert, and then go online for further details.

Web addresses – have a guess

If you can't find an organization's web address (sometimes also known as a Uniform Resource Locator, or URL, by the way), you can always try guessing it. Of course it doesn't work every time, but, with practice, it's surprising how often it does. It would certainly be worth trying this technique to find out whether Marks & Spencer has a site that gives its pretax profit. Some possible guesses might be:

- www.marks&spencer.com
- www.m&s.co.uk
- www.marksandspencer.com
- www.marks-and-spencer.com
- www.marks_and_spencer.co.uk

If you do guess, you also need to know what domain to try – the bit that indicates the type of organization. These are some of the commonest:

- .ac or .edu (educational establishments)
- .co (companies)
- .com (global commercial sites)
- .gov (government departments and agencies)
- .int (international organizations)
- .mus (museums)
- .net (network administrative bodies)
- .org (associations, professional bodies, organizations)
- .sch (schools)

A few addresses don't include a domain; the British Library's web address, for example, is simply www.bl.uk. Sites of international organizations obviously don't have a country code – and nor do United States sites. However, most web addresses do specify the geographic location, so this is the last element you need to consider when working out what a web address is likely to be. British sites have .uk and it's not too difficult to work out the rest – although they're not always what you might at first expect. Here are a few examples.

- .au (Australia)
- .ch (Switzerland)
- .de (Germany)
- .eu (European Union)
- .fr (France)
- .nl (Holland)

Using the web like a professional

Although anyone can use the web with very little introduction, it takes skill to use it well. Your job as a professional is to ensure that you can help your enquirers by being able to achieve better search results than they can manage by simply relying on Google. The web is now such a fundamental tool for enquiry answering that it's worth taking some time out to learn how to use it properly. Facet Publishing (the imprint of CILIP: the Chartered Institute of Library and Information Professionals) publishes a number of titles on internet use – not just the web, which is merely the multimedia part of the net. So check Facet's online catalogue at www.facetpublishing.co.uk to see what might be useful for you.

Finally, don't forget to add the useful sites you find to your list of favourites – either temporarily for the purposes of the current enquiry, or permanently as part of your library or information service's useful information file. Be disciplined about arranging your favourites logically too. There's nothing more frustrating than not being able to find the wonderful site you were using only yesterday.

Rapid reading

You can't always rely on printed sources having an index. And, even if there is a suitable searchable archive database for your purposes, you may not be able to afford to use it. So there will be times when you find yourself having to scan and browse rapidly through the text of an actual document or web page. You might need to look at a selection of articles, a set of news headlines, a bulky report or a chapter of an inadequately indexed book. If this happens, you certainly don't have to read every word. There are techniques that you can learn for rapid and efficient reading, and it's a good idea to practise them. Some of the commonest ones are:

- Look at the document's signposting first: title; subtitle; standfirst; executive summary; conclusions, findings or recommendations; section headings; bullet points; lists; boxes; captions.

Then…

- Read down the middle of the page, relying on your peripheral vision to spot significant words. (How do you know what those words are going to be? You use your mini-thesaurus.)
- Alternatively, if you're faced with long lines of print, bounce your eye from the left hand to the right hand side of the page.

Look in addition for the following elements, which will be easy to spot because they stand out from the rest of the text, and also offer the best clues as to the document's content:

- Capitalized words (likely to be the names of organizations, people or concepts)
- Abbreviations (shortened forms of those names)
- Numerals (whatever they are measuring will also give you valuable clues as to the document's relevance to your enquiry)
- Any words in non-standard typography – e.g. bold, italic or small caps.

And – a first rate technique for getting through longer documents really quickly . . .

- Read the first sentence of each paragraph and ignore all the rest.

This isn't really 'rapid reading', of course. You're just reading at your normal reading speed. The trick is knowing what *not* to read. And it only works if you already have a pretty clear idea of what you're looking for. Your eye won't instinctively spot a significant word or phrase unless you've already worked out what those words or phrases are. So constructing your own mini-thesaurus is just as important for browsing and scanning as it is for using indexes. And one final tip: if the text you have to read is on a screen, print it out first. The screen flickers, the lights flicker, and the resolution is probably clearer in print anyway. So give your eyes a break by making it as easy as possible for them to spot what you're looking for.

Coming next – meeting deadlines every time...

All of this searching takes time, and you start out with no guarantee of success. So what do you do when you realize that time is running out and you're no nearer an answer than you were when you started? In Chapter 6, we'll look briefly at efficient time management, which can allow you to meet deadlines every time.

To recap . . .

- Decide whether to go for the most up-to-date, most relevant or most appropriate source first.
- Beware of variant spellings, homonyms, and British versus American terminology.
- Construct your own mini-thesaurus before you start searching.
- Be ready to change your search strategy (and amend your mini-thesaurus) in the light of what you find.
- Exploit the web – using search engines, following links and guessing web addresses.
- Learn and practise rapid reading techniques for scanning and browsing.

CHAPTER 6

Quick! Time's running out

How to meet deadlines every time

In this chapter you'll find out how to:

- **distinguish between vital and urgent tasks**
- **establish a working timetable**
- **compromise on the answer**
- **provide progress reports.**

Internet service providers have a lot to answer for. How many times have you seen poster or magazine ads with phrases like 'A world of information at your fingertips'? The trouble is that enquirers believe them. They really do think that you can now find anything you want with just a few deft mouse clicks. The web has it all. And you can get at it instantly.

E-mail and fax haven't helped either. Once upon a time, dealing with written enquiries did at least give you a breathing space, in which you could agree a realistic deadline that allowed you to work out a sensible search strategy, including making provision for things going wrong. Nowadays, though, enquirers know that they can have a written answer instantly; blaming delays on the post is no longer an option. Actually there are many positives to this; as we discussed in Chapter 1, e-mail does allow you to maintain that vital dialogue with the enquirer, even if they're on the other side of the world. But there's no doubt that improvements in telecommunications are encouraging enquirers to demand ever tighter deadlines.

You can't really blame enquirers for believing they can have it all instantly. But you must manage their expectations, and you must then deliver what you promise. So how can you do this? The first thing is to maintain a positive attitude, keep a clear head, and distinguish between what's vital and what's urgent.

Vital versus urgent

We discovered in Chapter 1 that 'urgent' is not an acceptable deadline for any enquiry. You need to know *how* urgent; you need a date and/or a time. Now we need to take that a stage further and make sure that we really understand what we mean by urgency.

Faced with a limited amount of time and a number of competing tasks, you need first of all to sort them into priority order and allocate time between them – and you need to revise that timetable constantly as new tasks come along to demand your attention. To do this, you need to be clear about the relative importance and difficulty of the tasks before you.

Let's deal with importance first. A 'vital' task is one without which your organization cannot function. An 'urgent' task is one which has an imminent deadline; it may or may not be vital. If you don't buy information sources, install, catalogue and index them, and learn how they work, then you can't answer the enquiries. So these are 'vital' tasks. But they're not necessarily 'urgent'; if you put them off until tomorrow, no great harm may be done. They may in due course become urgent. If you're constantly being asked for information that's sitting in a document that you haven't yet catalogued, or a piece of software that you haven't yet installed, then that cataloguing or installation becomes not only 'vital' but also 'urgent'. Let's see how it might apply to enquiry work.

First come first served?

You have three urgent enquiries to do. They all have the same deadline. But one is for a colleague doing a college course on day release, another is for your boss and the third is for a client of your organization. Your job is to answer enquiries for all these three people, so they're all vital; if you don't do them, you'll be in trouble. But if you fail your colleague you'll probably just get ticked off; if you fail the boss you might lose your job, and if you fail the client, everyone might lose their jobs. So you can see that there are degrees of urgency, depending on how vital the task is. You might deal with it by:

- **firstly** suggesting an appropriate source for the colleague to use for him or herself,
- **secondly** warning the boss that you're doing an enquiry for a client and either providing a brief 'holding' answer for the boss or negotiating a longer deadline (or both), and then . . .
- **thirdly** concentrating on the client.

Once you've dealt with your competing enquiries in the manner outlined above, you can then work out how long you need to allocate to each. Five minutes with the catalogue or a couple of other finding aids may be enough for your college colleague, and 15 minutes looking up and downloading or photocopying a few pieces of information will put the boss on the back burner for a while. This leaves you the rest of the morning to spend doing database searches, scanning journal references and compiling a list of addresses for the client. (And preparing to present the answer in a helpful way; we'll look at adding value in Chapter 8.)

Of course, it doesn't work like this in a busy reference or educational library. There every enquirer is equally important, and you have to employ different techniques to ensure that everyone's deadlines are met. To do this, you really need to be able to assess instantly the relative difficulty of answering each enquiry, and the amount of time you'll need to devote to it. There's probably no easy way of doing this; it comes with experience and, even then, you'll still encounter some enquiries that turn out to be almost impossible to answer, even though you thought they were going to be easy. But you can help yourself by making sure that you do know your basic reference sources really well – just a strictly limited number of them, such as the ones listed at the front of this book. If you are familiar with their contents, then you should know what's feasible and where you're going to have to negotiate with the enquirer about providing a compromise answer.

Time is money

Difficulty doesn't necessarily equate to time (although it might). An alternative to spending time on a difficult enquiry might be to use a charged-for database, where the time saved justifies the expense. Assuming that you've correctly identified the right one to use, searchable archive databases can save you an enormous amount of time – not least because they *fail* as quickly as they *succeed*. Just think about it for a moment. If you use printed sources, it takes you longer to fail to find the answer than it does to succeed because, once you've found it, you stop looking. Whereas if you keep not finding it, you go on looking until you've exhausted every possibility. A database, on the other hand, fails as quickly as it succeeds by telling you instantly that there's nothing available on your chosen subject, so you know much further ahead of the deadline that an enquiry is going to be difficult, and you still have time to do something about it.

The moral here is that time is money. Whether you choose to spend money on an online search that takes five minutes, or restrict yourself to 'free' printed sources or the web and spend an hour looking things up or surfing instead, the result is the same – cost to your organization. In making efficient use of your time, and deciding when to call a halt and compromise on the answer instead, you must always bear in mind that every minute you spend on an enquiry is costing your organization money. It's not just the cost of your modest salary either, or the online or copying charges; there are overheads to take into account as well – things like lighting, heating, rent and rates, to say nothing of the cost of acquiring and managing all your information sources in the first place. The less efficiently you plan your search strategy, the more it costs your organization.

Your working timetable

We've already done some assessment of the relative difficulty of our sample enquiries. Assuming that they all have the same deadline (and that your library or information service has all the sources necessary for answering them), let's see what this is likely to mean for our timetabling.

I'm looking for information on migration patterns in Wales
Verdict: A very small quantity of looking up – on the Office for National Statistics website or in a statistical digest – should tell you that the Census is the place to look. But, whether you use it in electronic or printed form, the Census is a huge document. So this enquiry is fairly **easy** but could be a bit **slow**.

I'm trying to find a song called When I would sing under the ocean [but the title is probably wrong]
Verdict: The trouble with this enquirer's Chinese whisper is that you're starting off looking for something that doesn't exist, and then when you've realized that, you haven't a clue what the real title is. So this enquiry could be very **hard** and also **slow**. (Of course, once you do know the correct title, then there are plenty of lists, catalogues and websites of songs to check it in; so the final stages will probably turn out to be fairly easy and quite quick).

Do you have the electoral register?
Verdict: It will probably take only a minute or two to check that the enquirer really does want the current register for the local area. Assuming they do, and

that you're working in a public library, then you'll have it. If you're not, then you'll at least know who to phone to check it. So this enquiry is very **easy**, fairly **quick**.

What is Marks & Spencer's current pretax profit?
Verdict: This enquiry is **easy** because there are plenty of places where the figure could be found, and should be very **quick** if you use the web.

I'm looking for information on who's doing research into the health risks of artificial and natural radiation, and it's worth searching elsewhere if we don't find the article I remember from New Scientist
Verdict: Your enquirer didn't help to start with by just asking for one source when what they probably needed was a fairly extensive literature search. There are at least plenty of sources providing references to scientific literature – albeit frequently charged-for services – although it may take a little time to find suitable articles from them. So this enquiry will probably turn out to be fairly **easy** but a bit **slow**.

I'm doing a project on the Westminster Aquarium
Verdict: Once you've interpreted this enquirer's muddle, you'll probably find that the answer requires a lot of looking up for not much information. So this one will be **hard** and **slow**.

Cash for Parliamentary questions... Strong & Moral Britain Association... neofascist organizations... funding... school governors... declarations of interest
Verdict: This is a very big job; it's probably going to involve looking things up, searching printed and electronic sources and phoning round. You might be able to speed some parts of it up by using databases, but there are so many aspects to it, and some of them are so speculative, that it's still going to take a long time. So it's pretty **hard** and very **slow**. However, you could look at it another way and say that the only bit of this three-part query that really matters is what interests school governors have to declare – in which case it could become quite a bit **easier** and **quicker**.

Finally, then, let's use these assessments to sort the enquiries into priority order, so that everybody gets started as quickly as possible.

1 *What is Marks & Spencer's current pretax profit?* (Very easy, very quick.)

2 *Do you have the electoral register?* (Easy and probably quick.)

3 *I'm looking for information on who's doing research into the health risks of artificial and natural radiation.* (Fairly easy, but could be slow.)

4 *I'm looking for information on migration patterns in Wales.* (Fairly easy but could well be slow.)

5 *I'm doing a project on the Westminster Aquarium.* (Hard and slow, but at least you can leave the enquirer browsing.)

6 *Cash for Parliamentary questions... Strong & Moral Britain Association... neo-fascist organizations... funding... school governors... declarations of interest.* (Hard and slow, and the enquirer will probably need a lot of help.)

7 *I'm trying to find a song called* 'When I would sing under the ocean' [*but the title is probably wrong*]. (Until you discover the correct title, this is going to be very hard and is probably going to require you to do quite a lot of asking around on the enquirer's behalf, so it will be very slow too.)

Beware! This is not the right order for everyone. People's perception of difficulty varies depending on their experience and the environment they work in. (A music librarian might put the '*Sing under the ocean*' mystery right at the top of the list, for example, because at least they ought to be able to come up with plenty of ideas for tackling it.) So you should take this section as a guide to technique, not as the answer to the problem.

If you're actually doing all the enquiries yourself, your chosen order of priority means that you can start getting answers out from the earliest possible moment. If you're simply helping the enquirers to find the answers for themselves, then this strategy means that everyone gets started as rapidly as possible and you have time to monitor everybody's progress and help wherever necessary.

A compromise answer?

But, unfortunately, even this can't guarantee success. It may be that you really have more to do than you can possibly manage in the time available. In that case, you could find yourself having to compromise on the answer. Do avoid ever saying 'no' if you possibly can, but you have to accept that there will be times when you need to say 'yes – but . . .'. The important thing is to try to advance on all fronts – leave everybody with something, rather than some with a complete answer and others with nothing. There are various things you can do to keep to your deadlines.

Suggest sources rather than finding answers

Suggesting sources in which your enquirer can look, rather than finding the answer for them, is an obvious tactic, and enquirers are usually sympathetic if they can see that you're under pressure from other people standing round. But it can be harder to convince them that you are short of time if there's no-one else around, no matter how many jobs you are working on for absent enquirers. And don't expect to get any sympathy if you actually list for the enquirer's edification all the other things you have to do – that's your problem, not theirs. If you do have to resort to suggesting sources, make sure that you explain fully to the enquirer how the source works; show them the different indexes available in a printed source, take them through the various menus or buttons on a database or website. And invite them to return for further advice if the source doesn't work; don't ever give the impression that you're fobbing them off.

Suggest alternative libraries or information services

Suggesting sources doesn't work with telephone or e-mail enquirers. If you can't help them immediately, you could suggest an alternative library or information service that they could try. But again, be as helpful as possible in doing this. Look up the organization's phone number, e-mail address and website in a directory, and tell your enquirer exactly what that library/information service can do that you can't. In some cases, merely giving an e-mail enquirer the web address of a relevant institution may be sufficient in itself – especially if its site has a good Frequently Asked Questions (FAQs) section. Beware, though, of directing enquirers to services that they are not entitled to use. Some institutions will accept enquiries only from their members or subscribers; others will want to charge.

Ask for thinking time

An alternative tactic when dealing with telephone or e-mail enquirers is to say 'Leave it with me; I'll see what I can do.' This buys you valuable time and leaves the enquirer satisfied that you are taking the enquiry seriously. However, you must take the time straight away to go through the full questioning procedure that we discussed in Chapter 1. You must also agree a deadline with the enquirer – and then meet it.

Offer a 'quick & dirty' answer

Of course, asking for thinking time merely leaves you with yet another deadline to meet. In that case, an alternative tactic is to offer an instant but partial answer, based on what you have immediately to hand. (This tactic works equally well whether the enquirer is standing in front of you or has got in touch by phone, e-mail or fax.) A quick & dirty answer is usually a briefer one – whatever you can find in a few minutes in readily accessible sources. However there are some occasions when a quick & dirty answer can be a longer one. It might take only a few minutes to do a rough and ready web or database search and hand the results over unchecked for the enquirer to go through in detail in their own time. Whereas, if you had the time yourself, you would take personal responsibility for going through the downloaded results and removing the less relevant material. (This is all part of adding value, and we'll return to it in Chapter 8.)

Progress reports

Whatever strategies you choose to employ to ensure you meet your deadlines, it's important to keep enquirers informed on how you're getting on. You're likely to do this automatically when the enquirer is standing over you, but you should get into the habit of doing it for absent enquirers too. It's reassuring to the enquirer, and it shows them that you're being open about any difficulties and not trying to pull the wool over their eyes. And, although you'll always hope to succeed in finding the answer, progress reports can also prepare enquirers for disappointment (and put them in a mood for accepting a compromise answer) if your searching is going badly. Making progress reports may seem irksome and time-consuming, but it undoubtedly pays customer relations dividends.

Coming next – what to do if you can't find the answer...

All of this assumes, of course, that you actually have some hope of finding the answer. But what do you do if it's just nowhere to be found? In Chapter 7, we'll think about what to do if your chosen sources fail to come up with the answer at all.

To recap . . .

- **Make sure you understand the difference between vital and urgent tasks.**
- **Establish a working timetable, grading and prioritizing enquiries according to whether they are easy or hard, quick or slow.**
- **Buy time if necessary by supplying sources instead of doing the searching, or suggesting alternative institutions, or asking for thinking time, or offering a quick & dirty answer.**
- **Always keep your enquirers informed about progress.**

CHAPTER 7

Can't find the answer – what now?

What to do if your chosen sources fail

> **In this chapter you'll find out how to:**
>
> ■ **prepare your enquirer for disappointment**
> ■ **settle for an alternative answer**
> ■ **look for outside help**
> ■ **decide whether it's worth buying the information in.**

You've done everything you should have done: quizzed the enquirer about their real needs; imagined the final answer; assessed the subject for focus, dynamism and complexity; searched systematically using a mini-thesaurus – and drawn a blank at every turn. Is it the end of the road? Certainly not – although you are now probably going to have to rethink the task and discuss alternative strategies with your enquirer.

Sometimes you can anticipate this difficulty. If you work in a specialist information unit and a regular user happens to ask you something outside your organization's core business, then you'll probably know straight away that you don't have the resources to answer it in-house. You may even be able to judge that the enquiry is so esoteric and so specific that it might not be in a published source at all, and that locating expert advice is the only solution.

If you do suspect from the outset that you're going to have difficulty answering a particular enquiry, then there's a fourth characteristic that you have to consider in addition to focus, dynamism and complexity: viability.

Saying 'no' positively

With so much information now available, both online and in print, is there any excuse for failing to find an answer? Sometimes. Your enquirer may decide that the information is just not worth the cost of using a charged-for online service or hiring an independent information professional. You may decide that you can't afford to invest the time on a speculative and possibly fruitless attempt to find a website that might be able to help. So, no matter how much technology you surround yourself with, and no matter how well funded your organization is, there are times when you might still have to admit defeat.

But even this doesn't mean saying 'no'. It means exercising ingenuity in helping your enquirer to continue travelling hopefully instead of hitting a *cul de sac*. It means thinking positively about what you can still do. Remember the technique you used when your mind went blank in Chapter 3? You said 'I'm sure I can help', and indeed you still can – although by now not necessarily in the way your enquirer expected.

Preparing your enquirer for disappointment

So it's probably just as well to start lowering your enquirer's expectations as soon as you realize there are going to be difficulties. This is where the progress reports mentioned in Chapter 6 come in. You'll be in a much better position to help your enquirer if they're already aware that you are having problems and are starting to think about what alternative answers would be acceptable.

What you can do to save the situation at this stage will depend on what exactly your enquirer wants the information for. As we discovered in Chapter 2, people rarely want information merely to satisfy idle curiosity – they nearly always have a purpose in asking. This means that you can sometimes accommodate their needs by providing an alternative answer – less specific than the one they asked for, for example, but almost as helpful in enabling them to reach the conclusion they seek or put forward the argument they want to promote. To decide where to look for this, you need to go back to the technique we looked at in Chapter 3, and try to imagine the appearance not of an ideal answer but of an acceptable alternative.

Where else can you go?

If you don't have anything in-house that might provide the answer, then you can always seek outside help. This offers you lots of scope; there are thousands of sources you could consider, and plenty of places you can look to identify them. As we saw in Chapter 6, providing the web address of a relevant institution may offer your enquirer some immediate help. Beyond this, though, seeking outside help usually imposes delays on the answer and, as we again saw in Chapter 6, you frequently don't discover that you're in difficulties until the deadline is looming. So, a third possibility is to use a charged-for database to find the information. This can at least speed the process up, and produce some results, however sketchy and incomplete. But it can also be expensive, and your enquirer would presumably have to bear the cost.

The really important thing at this stage is to keep your enquirer informed. You have to be realistic about it; you are the bearer of bad news, and your job now is to soften its impact. You need further help from your enquirer on what would be an acceptable way of salvaging the enquiry, so you need to go right back to the kinds of questions and answers that we looked at in Chapter 1 – almost a repeat of the original dialogue, but with a changed agenda.

Of course, you might have anticipated the difficulties, using the easy/hard and quick/slow assessments that we looked at in Chapter 6. And you will of course have decided (as we discussed in Chapter 4) whether to go for the most up to date, most relevant or most appropriate sources first. So you may well be quite clear what your next move must be, without any further reference to your enquirer. But warn them, nevertheless.

Looking for outside help

There are hundreds of possible sources that can lead you to outside help on every conceivable topic, and you will be very unlucky indeed if you can't find anywhere at all to direct your enquirer to. (Have another look at the 25 multi-purpose reference sources at the front of this book; *most* of them can lead you to further sources of help.) Seeking outside help also has the advantage of sticking to the enquirer's agenda, whereas if you suggest a substitute answer, you inevitably shift the agenda to suit you. But going outside does introduce a further delay, and it also means that you can no longer necessarily guarantee the attention and courtesy that you are of course giving your own enquirer. Remember, an unsatisfactory response from a contact that you have recommended can rebound on you.

The Westminster Aquarium enquiry is an ideal candidate for referral. Frustrated at your failure to find anything that provides any detail on what must at first have seemed to be a fairly straightforward topic, you do at least know from its name roughly where the building was. You will also be aware

– or could speculate – that local history and archive services are a local authority responsibility, and will be able to look up the relevant authority and locate its archives service. This just about the simplest and most straightforward referral you can do.

But it's not the only kind. You might draw a complete blank with the Strong & Moral Britain Association. If it's the kind of organization your enquirer suspects, with neo-fascist connections, then it might not be particularly forthcoming with information about itself for publication in directories or on the web. So that's when you might need to exercise a bit of imagination and think what kinds of alternative sources would be interested in helping. Faced with this situation, there's another hypothetical question you need to ask yourself – and that question is:

Who really needs to know this?

In this case, anti-racist organizations seem the obvious candidates; a quick check of a source like the *Directory of British Associations* would reveal the Institute of Race Relations as one possible candidate, and would tell you whether it had a library or offered an information service.

If you're in the habit of using specialist e-mail discussion lists, then you can of course consider contacting the members of an appropriate list for help. Posting to a discussion list has the advantage of putting the problem before a large number of people; and it only needs one person to have experience of dealing with the same or a similar enquiry in the past for most of your troubles to be over. It may be your only hope in your quest for a song called *When I would sing under the ocean*; no reference sources are going to reveal it under this title, so you may be completely reliant on a musical colleague with a crossword puzzle mentality making the connection. Don't just take their answer at face value, though, no matter how grateful you are; tactfully double-check the information by looking up *When I was king of the Beotians* in an encyclopedia of music, a recordings catalogue, a book of operettas, or perhaps a music search or file-sharing site.

If informal discussion lists don't work, you can actually use the web to ask other libraries for help. Enquire, Discover & Read is an initiative, managed in the UK by the People's Network, to provide 24/7 library and information services to the public. The Enquire part of the service (www.peoplesnetwork. gov.uk/enquire) connects you via an online enquiry form to a library and information professional in either the UK, USA or Canada (depending on the time of day) who will take your query, investigate and respond either by e-mail or by live chat link. Be very careful not to abuse such a service, though. Remember, enquiry answering is your job and there's no excuse for becoming lazy!

Asking authors or editors

You can use the results of your literature searching for a third type of referral – to the authors of nearly relevant books or articles, or the editors of what seem like appropriate journals. Your hunt for material on the Westminster Aquarium may have led you to a lovely coffee-table book on Victorian pleasure palaces, with just one picture of the Aquarium and a brief caption. So why not try contacting the author? You might find them in one of a number of Who's Who type publications that cover writers, but sources of this kind are always highly selective in who they include, and are not always particularly up-to-date; so an alternative would be to use the book's publisher as a go-between. Actually this isn't an ideal solution either, because professional authors (as opposed to enthusiasts) are often reluctant to enter into correspondence, and publishers tend to be protective of their authors too. A better alternative might be to scrutinize the bibliography to see if it can lead you to more detailed literature that your enquirer might be able to see in a specialist library, or borrow through the British Library's document supply service.

Contacting authors of articles in specialist journals, or the editors of those journals, can be more fruitful. Driven by their own enthusiasm, they may be more committed to their subject than a jobbing author or commercial book publisher would be. In the Westminster Aquarium enquiry, the classified index to *Willing's Press Guide* ('Consumer: other classifications: historic buildings') reveals the existence of a magazine called *The Victorian*, whose coverage includes 'architecture and social history of the period'. Alternatively, a search in *Directory of British Associations* will reveal the existence of over 20 organizations under 'Architecture: history & preservation'. The website of one of them – the Victorian Society (www.victorian-society.org.uk) – shows that it is the publisher of *The Victorian*, and that the theme of the July 2001 issue actually was 'Iron and Glass: the influence of the Crystal Palace'. Whether or not it mentions the Aquarium remains to be seen – but it's certainly worth following up.

Buying the information in

When you've exhausted all these possibilities, there may be no alternative to buying the information in. You'd not only be buying time that you were not able to devote to the enquiry yourself, but probably also some kind of expertise in the subject concerned. For example, if you or your enquirer were unhappy about the authoritativeness and quality of the information you could find on the web about research into the health effects of radiation, you could perhaps contact the Association of Independent Information Professionals (www.aiip.org) to find an online researcher who could search specialist science, technology and medical databases on your behalf.

This can be an expensive option, of course; you'd be paying every penny of the researcher's costs, plus their profit. Costly as it may seem in cash terms, using a commercial online service would almost certainly work out cheaper (assuming, that is, that you were a reasonably efficient searcher who worked out their strategy beforehand and found useful content relatively quickly). When looking for the kind of investigative coverage you need to flush out the Strong & Moral Britain Association, for instance, an extensive full text news and articles retrieval service, such as LexisNexis, or an online library of periodical articles, such as the web version of *British Humanities Index* or the British Library's Direct or Inside services, may be essential.

Expensive commercial online?

In real terms, commercial online services are actually becoming cheaper. This is partly because of technological developments, which mean that the prices charged by the existing commercial services have risen by less than the rate of inflation over the years, but it's also because of the available range of pricing packages. If you're likely to be a heavy user of services such as Dialog or LexisNexis, then you'd go for a fixed price package involving a substantial payment up-front with effectively unlimited use thereafter.

Alternatively, pricing packages based on the amount of content you retrieved and downloaded would enable you to cherry-pick information as required, perhaps paying for it online with a corporate credit card. Obviously the unit cost of the information you purchased would be higher than if you took out a blanket subscription, but the service wouldn't be costing you a penny when you weren't using it. These are decisions that you will have to take when you're planning the kind of information service most appropriate for your organization. (We'll return to this in Chapters 9 and 10.)

Settling for an alternative answer

After you've reviewed all these other options, there's probably nothing else left now but to suggest an alternative answer. Let's have a think about possible substitute answers to a couple of our sample enquiries. There just might not be enough time to undertake a full analysis of all the migration figures for Wales from the Census. But the Office for National Statistics (ONS) website should have led you to *Regional Trends*, an annual digest that includes some population figures for Wales and its surrounding English regions including a couple of short tables of migration figures. Would this be acceptable, given the time available? That would be for your enquirer to decide.

The Westminster Aquarium enquiry is likely to prove particularly frustrating. It will probably take you ages to pull together a pathetic little selection of references. If you've managed a brief entry in an encyclopaedia of London, an illustration from a book of Victorian views, a few sentences gleaned from the indexes of textbooks and the odd web page that doesn't really tell you anything new, then you'll have done very well indeed. But remember your enquirer told you that they were doing a project – for school or college, one assumes. They need enough material for a 500-word essay, so what can you add?

Bearing in mind your earlier discovery of the Victorian Society, you could suggest broadening the scope of the project to take in some of the context in which the Westminster Aquarium operated. Perhaps it could also cover other popular Victorian entertainment venues in London, or social studies on the growth of working-class wealth and leisure during the nineteenth century. There should be plenty of material on both these topics – indeed, you'll already be in a position to recommend suitable sources, because you've already come across them while actually looking for references to the Aquarium. Your hapless enquirer, whose own deadline will undoubtedly be tight (students only seem to come to a library and information professional for help at the last moment) will probably fall upon you with gratitude. But beware! You've changed the agenda in this enquiry to suit yourself; so be especially sensitive to your enquirer's reaction, to make sure that the suggested change also suits them. Your enquirer will not be impressed if you try to present an alternative answer as a lovely surprise.

Coming next – adding value...

Let's continue on a more positive note. This book is about success, after all. But successful enquiry answering doesn't simply mean handing the answer over with no further comment. It's about making sure that what you provide is the best available, presented to your enquirer in the most helpful way possible. So in the next chapter, we'll look at how to add value to your answers.

> **To recap . . .**
>
> ■ **Keep your enquirer informed of difficulties, so that you can both be thinking of acceptable alternative answers.**
> ■ **Look for specialist organizations, authors and bibliographies of nearly relevant literature, and editors of appropriate journals, as possible sources to refer your enquirer to.**
> ■ **Consider using independent information professionals or commercial online services, bearing in mind cost versus value.**
> ■ **Make sure that any less detailed or broader substitute answer that you provide still addresses your enquirer's needs.**

CHAPTER 8

Success! Now let's add some value

Presenting your answer well is part of the job

> **In this chapter you'll find out how to:**
>
> ■ **make sure that you really have answered the question**
> ■ **decide what to leave out of the answer**
> ■ **take time and trouble over presenting what's left – orally, visually.**

There can scarcely be a library or information service in the world that believes it is over-funded. More often than not, the staff feel that they're struggling with inadequate resources, and that there simply aren't enough of them to satisfy the demands placed upon the services they provide. That's why the emphasis throughout this book has been on using moderately priced mainstream information sources, and on getting a quart out of a pint pot. Where we have referred to high-priced commercial services, it has always been on the assumption that they are a medium of last resort.

But you can still take pride in the answers you provide. This is partially for your personal satisfaction, but it's also really good customer relations. A service that looks and sounds good inspires customer confidence and wins repeat business; one that doesn't risks losing that confidence, resulting in declining business and possibly even closure. In helping people find the information they want, you haven't been doing something easy, you've been doing something highly skilled. So don't spoil it by presenting the answer sloppily.

Have you really answered it?

But before you present the answer at all, do make sure that you really have answered the question. Go back to your enquiry form, notebook, log, enquiry management system or whatever you use in your library or information service, and check the wording carefully. Do this for two reasons – firstly, because you waste your enquirer's time if you find that you've allowed yourself to be unconsciously diverted during the course of your researches. (Remember your exams again – there are no marks for submitting the perfect answer to a question that isn't on the paper.)

Secondly, you need to check because enquirers are quite capable of changing the agenda while you are searching, without bothering to tell you. Remember the problems you encountered in Chapter 1, trying to find out what your enquirers really wanted in the first place? Unfortunately, it doesn't stop there. While you are busy trying to find the answer, your enquirer is still thinking about the question, and probably coming up with all sorts of supplementary information that they'd like as well. Or they may have been pursuing their own researches in parallel to yours, and have already come up with the answer to the question they originally put to you. Annoying as this may be, you have to be tolerant. After all, it's just a job for you, but it might be personally very important for them.

What to leave out

We worried about information overload as early as Chapter 2. But it's now, while you're preparing to present your answer, that it really matters. You may well have found similar information from several different sources. This could be because you were unhappy with the level of detail in the first source you used, and wanted to see whether you could improve on it in another one. Or because you found several articles or news items on the same subject, with huge overlaps between them. Or half a dozen different organizations that you could refer your enquirer to, because you hadn't been able to find the information in-house.

But there's no rule that says you have to provide them all. As the quantity of available information continues to grow, enquirers will be looking to library and information professionals for their expertise not only in finding the right answer but also in judging which is the best *version* of the right answer. All information work is about choices – choosing what sources to buy, choosing what index entries to create for them, choosing what to leave out when you write abstracts of them. Why should enquiry work be any different?

Information versus references

Of course, there will be times when you genuinely don't feel well qualified enough to make decisions of this kind – in highly technical subjects such as medicine or law, for instance. But even then you can still opt for offering complete texts of only some of the sources, and providing references to the others. That way, you've minimized the amount that your enquirer has to read and, if you've been providing your answer on paper, using photocopies or downloads of key sources (subject to prevailing copyright rules, of course), then you've also been kind to trees.

Whatever you do decide to provide, you should always tell your enquirer where the information has come from. It may be tempting to keep these details to yourself, in a misguided attempt to ensure that the enquirer remains dependent on you. But resist the temptation. Firstly, it's a very unprofessional practice for one whose job is providing information from public domain sources. Secondly, it's all too easy for an enquirer to go to another library or information service that is prepared to source its information. And thirdly, if your enquirer subsequently comes back for further details, it's extremely embarrassing if you can't remember where the information came from in the first place.

Presenting what's left

So you've found the right answer – perhaps presented in several different ways – and you've decided which version is the best one for your enquirer's purposes. Now all you have to do is hand it over in triumph. So just take a few moments to decide how you're going to do it. After all, you don't want to spoil the climax, do you?

If you're presenting the answer orally, make sure that what you tell your enquirer covers all the points – no less, no more – and warns of any complications or potential pitfalls. If you're responding by phone, remember too that it will probably take a few seconds for the person at the other end to get onto your wavelength. So use those few seconds to introduce yourself, say where you're calling from and remind the enquirer what they asked for. Then check that they've got a pen and paper handy. Then give them the answer. Something like . . .

> Hello, is that Mr Sampson? This is Delilah Milton from the Ghaza Mills Reference Library. You asked me to find Marks & Spencer's current pretax profit, and I have

the information for you if you're ready . . . The total operating profit for the year ended 31 March 2005 for the Marks & Spencer group was £618.5 million before taking exceptional items into account and £745.3 million after. The information comes from the company's own website, which you can find at www.marksand-spencer.com. They also announced half year profits of £308.2 million in November 2005. The last full year results were announced in May 2005, which suggests that the 2005-2006 figures could be out very soon. Would you like me to let you know when they appear?

Bear in mind that your enquirer may want to know what those exceptional items were, so make sure you know where to find the details elsewhere in the company's online annual report. Oh and, by the way, if you are on the phone, don't forget to smile.

Enhancing answers on paper

When you're presenting an answer on paper, your scope for adding value is enormously enhanced. Obviously if you're simply handing over an original publication, you'll show the enquirer the relevant passage or entry. So if you're supplying a photocopy for your enquirer to keep, or if you're faxing the information back, mark the crucial sections. Highlight the relevant paragraph with a marker pen. Put asterisks against the most useful entries in a directory. Draw a line down the required column or across the required row of a table of statistics. Put in an arrow head to point out the key component of a diagram. Circle the right place on a map. And, whatever else you do, make sure that the source of your document is clearly cited. Underline it if it's already printed there; write it in if not. And make sure that all the volume, part and page details are included. These are suggestions, of course, not hard and fast rules. But, as a general principle, do whatever you can to lead your enquirer to the information they want as rapidly and clearly as possible.

Many of your enquiries will probably be quick reference affairs, over and done with in a few minutes. But if you regularly carry out extended enquiry work, why not consider handing over the results in a professional presentation folder? For a fee-based enquiry service, quite a lavish pre-printed offering may well be appropriate – it could enhance the perceived value of the information far beyond the cost of the folder itself. But even for more modest offerings, it could well be worth slipping the papers into a clear plastic folder with a smart piece of stationery, bearing your organization's logo, as the top sheet. (And, of course, you'd always include a covering note inviting your enquirer to come back and discuss the outcome if they wished.) The cost of doing something like this is minuscule, the customer relations value immense.

Enhancing answers electronically

With information presented electronically, the number of ways you can enhance it is really limited only by your own imagination. Electronic delivery of answers to enquiries is likely to happen more and more as electronic versions of specialist publications replace print versions, as you take more information from the web, and as growing numbers of your enquirers are able to receive e-mails.

You can help your enquirer to make sense of a large body of **text** by adding headlines, subheadings and guiding, and by highlighting the key words or phrases in the text in bold or italic. Finding those key words or phrases is easy for you. Using the word search facility in your word processing program or web browser, it takes only a few seconds for you to add an enormous amount of value to the answer. Alternatively, you could copy key paragraphs out of the original text and paste them in at the head of your answer. This allows your enquirer both to take in the crucial information immediately, and also to read it in its proper context later on. (How do you know what to highlight? You use your mini-thesaurus as a guide.)

You can enhance **figures** in the same way. If you have downloaded some statistical information or other numeric data to a spreadsheet, then it need be the work of only a few minutes to add value by calculating an average or median for the figures retrieved, or expressing them as percentages for greater clarity, or ranking them. Or you can turn them into a graph, bar or pie chart. Make sure you really understand what you're doing, though. It's all too easy for simple mistakes in spreadsheet creation to render figures seriously misleading, if not downright wrong!

The exponential growth of the web has also enormously increased the value of **images** as sources of information. A picture is worth a thousand words, the cliché goes, and you can exploit this to the limit in your enquiry answering. You can drop images into word-processed documents, or even supply your answer as an audiovisual presentation or web page if you think that's more appropriate. And as with electronic text, you don't necessarily need to show the whole picture; if one detail is particularly important, crop it out of the main image, using image processing software or even simply the image formatting facility on your word processor or audiovisual presentation software.

A word of warning, though: if you are presenting your answers electronically, make sure your virus checking software is up to scratch. Your enquirer will not be pleased if your answer arrives complete with its very own infection.

Copyright, licensing, ethics

And another thing to beware: there are ethical considerations to bear in mind when manipulating text, numbers or images in this way. Be sure that you make it quite clear what you have done with the version of the document that you finally present to your enquirer, so that they are in no doubt as to how it varies from the original. (And, as always, make sure that you cite the source in full in your answer.) Copyright is a vital issue too. Before you engage in activity of this kind, be sure that you understand the terms on which the publication, data or software concerned has been supplied to you. If the licence forbids supply of copies to a third party then, no matter how much you may regret the missed opportunity, you must not do it.

As a general principle, in fact, you should make sure that you understand *all* the photocopying and downloading restrictions under which your library or information service operates before you start any enquiry work. There's plenty of help available if you need it; Facet Publishing (the imprint of CILIP: the Chartered Institute of Library and Information Professionals) produces a whole range of publications relating to copyright and other legal issues that can affect libraries and information services, so check their website www.facetpublishing.co.uk for details of titles that may help you. As copying in all media becomes easier and easier, publishers understandably become more and more vigilant about infringements. And nothing could be worse for your customer relations than promising something that the rules don't subsequently allow you to deliver.

Coming next – learning from each enquiry . . .

Your task is nearly over. But before you finally sign the enquiry off, there are some really useful lessons to be learned from it – plus quite possibly new information sources to consider and new services that you could introduce as a result. So in the next chapter, we're going to think about what we can learn from each completed enquiry.

To recap . . .

■ Check finally that you really have answered the question; it's all too easy to be diverted, or for enquirers to change their mind.

■ Remember that you don't necessarily have to supply everything you've found; supply the best and refer to the rest.

■ Make sure you cite sources for every piece of information you supply and, if necessary, indicate how it varies from the original.

■ Seize every opportunity to add value; compose your oral answers carefully, highlight key information on paper, enhance downloaded data.

■ Always make sure you operate within copyright and licensing requirements.

CHAPTER 9

Sign-off: what can we learn from this enquiry?

Using completed enquiries to develop your services

In this chapter you'll find out how to:

- **assess enquiry performance consistently and objectively**
- **review the sources you used with a view to developing new services**
- **ensure that you have the right tools for the future.**

Sir Winston Churchill famously said at a turning point in the Second World War: 'This is not the end. This is not even the beginning of the end. But it is perhaps the end of the beginning.' And so it is at this stage in your enquiry answering. You've sent the enquirer away satisfied, it's true. But have you done everything you can for your own information service and the facilities it could provide? You've just spent a lot of time working for the benefit of one person or organization – your enquirer. If you left it at that, then you could be missing an opportunity to turn that time spent into a really useful investment.

So take some time to review the completed enquiry. Assess it for its difficulty and the time it took. Look carefully at the sources and delivery media you used; there are likely to be some new ones, and you need to consider whether or not it might be worth purchasing or subscribing to them. You may possibly have contacted some useful new organizations as well; you'll need to decide how to record them so you can benefit from their expertise again in the future. The enquiry may even have suggested to you an entirely new service that you could offer as a result, in which case you will have a lot of thinking to do, deciding how best to introduce and manage it.

Completing an enquiry successfully isn't the end; it's the start of the next phase in your enquiry service. So let's look at some of these considerations in more detail . . .

How successful were you?

Just as we said in Chapter 1 that you mustn't accept a vague deadline, so you shouldn't tolerate an imprecise measure of success either. It's all too easy for a complacent colleague to record as 'successful' an enquiry that a more conscientious one might regard as only partially successful. Taken to its extreme, this could result in the more conscientious one ending up with a poorer annual appraisal report (and even a lower salary increase) than the complacent one, simply because they were more honest and realistic in recording their degree of enquiry answering success.

So instead, you should go for more objective measures of success. Take a look at section 9 of the model enquiry form that we've suggested on page xvi. It offers three measures of success – complete, partial or compromise.

'Complete' success

'Complete' success means that you have provided an answer that met the enquirer's needs in every respect; you covered all aspects of the question, and provided an answer that will enable them to make a recommendation, take a decision or take action. In the case of the cash-for-questions query, for example, this would mean that you had: found some useful news coverage of the cash-for-questions affair that either mentioned your enquirer's brother or specifically eliminated him; discovered how the Strong & Moral Britain Association was funded and whether or not it was associated with neo-fascist organizations; and been able to provide some authoritative guidelines on what obligations school governors faced regarding declaration of other interests. Anything less than this, and you would probably have to record the degree of success as 'partial'.

'Partial' success

'Partial' success means that you have been able to find some of what the enquirer wants, but not all. You may, for example, have come up with some figures on migration patterns in Wales which show general trends over a period for the whole Principality, but not necessarily the degree of detail that the enquirer would have liked – nothing on specific movements into and out of Glamorgan, for example. In this case, you've certainly provided an answer that will get the enquirer started, but not enough to enable them to finish their task to their satisfaction; so you've probably referred them to some-where else as well. (We'll deal with recording referrals in a moment.)

'Compromise'

'Compromise' means that you and the enquirer have together agreed on an answer that was not exactly what the enquirer wanted, but which is an accept-able alternative nevertheless. In the Westminster Aquarium query, for example, you may have agreed to supplement the paltry offering you could provide on the Aquarium itself with background on Victorian entertain-ments, or rival attractions of the period, just to enable the enquirer to complete their project to the satisfaction of the project supervisor. This is not an ideal outcome, and you must of course have agreed it with the enquirer. But it's about as close to an admission of failure as you should ever allow your enquiry service to come.

No success?

Note that there is no space for recording that you were unsuccessful; remem-ber the promise you gave when you were starting to think about how you would answer the enquiry back in Chapter 3? 'I'm sure I can help' was what you said – and so you can, even if you and the enquirer eventually had to compromise on what kind of answer would be acceptable. If you ever felt that you had to record an 'unsuccessful' result, then what that would really mean is that the enquiry isn't finished yet. (Note, too, that we haven't talked about referrals yet; we'll come back to those in a moment.)

How long did it take to answer?

Next, you need to record how long the enquiry took to answer. You'll need to consider whether the time it took was pretty much what you would have expected, or whether it took longer. If it did take longer, then was this because it was more difficult than you expected, or just more time-consuming? These are not necessarily the same thing, and it comes back to the easy/quick hard/slow decisions you had to take when you were deciding on the working timetable for prioritizing your enquiries (Chapter 6). For example, hard needn't necessarily mean slow; you may decide that it's going to be so diffi-cult to discover the Strong & Moral Britain Association's neo-fascist connections that you'll speed up the process by using a database rather than a manual search. On the other hand, you might have very easily have found masses of data on migration patterns in Wales, but turning it into a form that was acceptable to the enquirer might have taken an inordinate amount of time.

It is vitally important to know how long enquiries take to answer, because time is money, and if there's a pattern to the difficult and/or lengthy enquiries then that raises implications about the appropriateness and value of the sources and delivery media you're using. Perhaps you need to invest in something new – and maybe you'll be able to offer some useful new services as a result. (We'll come back to this a little later on.)

Did you meet the deadline?

Then you need to know whether you met the enquirer's deadline. There are only two possible answers to this – yes or no. Nothing else will do, and if you're recording a lot of 'No's in this box then, again, you need to do some serious thinking about why, and what you need to do to improve your 'Yes' score. If you had to negotiate more time (You didn't just present a late answer without warning the enquirer that that was going to happen, did you?), then you need to record your reasons – not just to get you off the hook but so you can decide what service improvements are needed to try to prevent it happening again. It may well be that the enquiry took a long time because you just didn't know what would be the best sources or delivery media to get you started. Well, now you do. So record them, and make use of what you have learned the next time a similar enquiry comes up. (We'll come back to this too in a moment.)

Did you have to refer the enquiry elsewhere?

If you recorded partial success or a compromise outcome, then that may well mean that you also referred the enquiry to another organization. This should trigger a whole range of questions about how your service might be able to change and develop as a result. If it's an organization that you have never used before then, firstly, how did you discover it? If it was in a directory, then does that mean that that directory is actually more useful than you might previously have imagined? Have you checked the new organization's website to find out what else it can offer? Is that site worth adding to your list of favourites for future reference? And, if so, where is the best place to put it in your favourites classification?

And what about the organization itself? When you contacted it (You did contact it, didn't you? You didn't just leave the enquirer to make a cold call?), were the staff both helpful and useful (not necessarily the same thing)? If they were both helpful and useful, did they help out of goodwill? Or does the organization have an agenda to pursue? If the former, then you should certainly be grateful, but shouldn't necessarily rely on that goodwill persisting if you keep going back to the same organization time and time again. At some point, you'll need to decide what kind of long term relationship you want to have with it (see below). If it has an agenda, then that's fine just as long as you're clear what that agenda is. If you went looking for expert help on the health effects of radiation, for example, you may get exactly the same information from both the Health Protection Agency and Friends of the Earth – but they would be likely to put radically different interpretations on that information. And things aren't always necessarily that clear cut. If you contact an industry or trade organization, for example, then you'll need to know whether it's on the producer or consumer side of the fence, or whether it represents employers or employees – something which may not necessarily be obvious from its name.

Melodramatic as it may seem, you'll also need to know whether the organizations you contact are discreet. If an enquirer approaches an organization on your advice, and subsequently finds themselves bombarded with unsolicited communications from it, then they're likely to be upset with you at the intrusion on their privacy and, quite possibly, the infringement of data protection regulations as well. And if your approach to the organization or – even worse – your enquirer's approach becomes public without your or their consent, then you're in even bigger trouble. You may of course have redress against the organization under data protection rules, but by that time the damage will have been done. So the moral is: check immediately that the organization handles all enquiries in confidence.

Assuming that your referral organization has passed all these tests, then you'll finally need to consider your long-term relationship with it. It may be a trade association or professional body that offers a charged-for enquiry or advice service, which you might consider subscribing to. This is a big decision, of course, with implications for your budget. So it's not to be undertaken lightly. But you can't undertake it at all unless you have recorded the enquiry properly in the first place.

Did you discover any useful new sources or delivery media?

It's not at all unusual to discover that a source you already have in stock but have never really had the time to get to know properly turns out to be ideal for a particular kind of enquiry that has always foxed you in the past. Multi-purpose sources such as *Whitaker's Almanac* are crammed with useful snippets of information that you wouldn't necessarily expect to find there and, ironically, your colleagues in smaller, less well resourced services are far more likely to know about them because they will have got into the habit of making the most of the limited range of sources at their disposal.

So when you do discover a useful new source – whether print or electronic – do make sure you have procedures in place for recording it properly. A good technique is your own organization's customized Frequently Asked Questions (FAQs) facility. The form it takes will depend on the nature of the searching aids you have already chosen to develop for your service. It could possibly just be a regularly updated list on paper that you keep at the enquiry desk, but this seems a less and less satisfactory solution when there are so many more effective and flexible methods you could employ. So consider instead creating an in-house database – whether using a database package or simply a word processor – that you can post to your organization's intranet. Instantly updatable at any time, it should also enable you to create automatic links to any websites or e-mail addresses you include in it.

Put it on your network drive, if you can – or, better still, on your intranet – so everybody in the organization can have access to it. (If it's just a file on your network drive, then you'll probably need to make it read-only, so that only you can make changes to it after due consideration of the value of any new entry you want to add, and so that you can be sure that the indexing of your FAQs facility remains up to standard. However, you could consider creating it as a wiki, thereby allowing other people in the organization to update and correct the information when necessary.

An intranet-based FAQs facility reflecting your stock and services could in fact turn out to be one of the most valuable services you could provide to your organization. It means that you can also include live links to internal sources of information or expertise within your organization, creating the beginnings of a knowledge management system in which your library or information service has seized the initiative. Does this mean that you are giving away trade secrets, and putting your service at risk as a result? No – quite the reverse. It means that you're constantly drawing your users' attention to your services, and demonstrating your expertise at the same time.

When you discover a new source that you don't actually have, then of course you have to consider whether it's worth purchasing or subscribing to. If you decide that it is, then you should consider which delivery medium would be most appropriate for you (see Chapter 4 for details) and you'll also need to examine any copyright or licensing requirements, to ensure that you are entitled to exploit it in the way you want (Chapter 8). If, for example, you intend to network the new source direct to your users throughout the organization, then there are likely to be cost implications, because licence fees often vary depending on how many desks you intend to network the service to.

Whether you have access to a corporate intranet and can provide a networked current awareness service, or whether you have to rely simply on a printed newsletter or even notices by the enquiry desk, you should always have procedures in place for telling both your colleagues and your users about new services that you can offer as a result of new sources acquired. And remember, too, that it should be that way round; the services should come first, not the sources or delivery media. Your enquirers aren't interested in sources, but in outcomes.

This can all take time that you may feel you can ill afford when there are immediate pressing enquiries to be answered. But do try to make time to investigate new sources and to make sure you are fully exploiting the ones you already have. It will pay enormous dividends, and will mean that you will be able to provide an even better enquiry service in the future.

Coming next – new job: where do you start?

Throughout this book so far, we've tended to assume that you're working in a multipurpose library or information unit serving a fairly large community – members of the public, students at a college or the staff of a public or private sector organization, for instance. If so, then you'll have colleagues to call on for help, guidance and moral support. But of course you may be a solo – a one person – operation, the only information professional in your organization. You may not be working in an established library or information service either, but facing the challenge of setting up your own enquiry service from scratch. On top of that, it might be a brand new job, with all your new users waiting for you to deliver. If this is your situation now, or if you're thinking of moving on from your present job to face that challenge in the future, then the final chapter of this book is devoted to you.

To recap . . .

- Try to quantify the degree of success achieved in each enquiry; don't settle for a subjective measurement.
- If you had difficulty in meeting the enquirer's deadline, think about sources or services that could help you answer a similar enquiry faster next time.
- If you referred the enquiry to another organization, consider how helpful it was, and whether you could use it again.
- Make sure you integrate any new sources discovered during the enquiry with your existing ones.
- Make sure your service always remains relevant to your organization's needs.

CHAPTER 10

New job: where do you start?

Applying your experience to developing a new information service

> **In this chapter you'll find out how to:**
>
> - discover what your users need
> - identify and choose sources and services that will meet their needs
> - exploit the sources you have invested in
> - raise the profile of your service through branding, promotion and customer care
> - get help and support when you need it.

It's your first day in the new job. You've beaten off stiff competition, convinced a tough interview panel that you're the best candidate for them, and you're thrilled at the confidence they've shown in you by appointing you.

Perhaps it's a complete change of career direction for you. Maybe you've left the technical back-up and colleagues' support of a large public, educational or corporate library for the challenge of a tiny information unit in a company or not-for-profit organization. Maybe you have a staff member to manage for the first time. Or maybe you're a solo – a one person – operation, responsible for everything from service development through budgeting and IT troubleshooting right down to making the tea. You may have inherited an existing service which has become run down because your predecessor left months ago. Or you might be the first information professional your organization has ever employed, and you have the task of providing an entirely new service from scratch.

Whatever your new circumstances, you're now the organization's information expert, and your new employer is looking to you to deliver. How on earth do you start?

Finding out what your users need

Fortunately, you won't be starting from a position of total ignorance. You will have prepared thoroughly for your interview by looking at the organization's website, reading its promotional literature and its annual report. You'll know the names of the senior people – possibly met one or two of them on your interview panel. And you will by now be thoroughly well versed in what the organization does and what its goals are. All of this is vital data in your quest for ways of making yourself indispensable.

When you finally arrive to start the job, what you need in addition is detailed intelligence on the information needs of the organization's key decision-makers. So your first priority should be to meet as many of them as possible at the earliest opportunity.

Meeting the top people

This may not be easy. Key decision-makers are by definition busy people, and they may not see the immediate benefit of setting aside time to be quizzed by you. They may even have fearsome PAs whose job is to protect them from approaches by people just like you. The important thing is not to let yourself be put off, although you may have to adopt a more subtle approach to secure the meetings you need.

However far down the hierarchy you feel yourself to be, there will be at least one or two more senior people to whom you do have an *entrée*: the ones who interviewed you. So approach them and ask them for introductions to their colleagues. If you do this, you'll probably get a sympathetic hearing – both from them and from the colleagues to whom they introduce you. Your interview panel members will already have had an opportunity to assess you, and compare you with other candidates, and will know that you're not a time-waster. Their reputation will be on the line too, because they will be the ones who have taken the decision to invest in you, and they will recognize that they must now help you to succeed. And the colleagues to whom they introduce you may well now be curious to meet this new addition to the organization, who comes with such a high recommendation.

Who to target

The first thing you need to do is to try to decide which of the organization's decision makers are likely to be the most in need of information. This will enable you to draw up a list of your top targets and tick them off as you meet them.

This isn't an exact science, of course, but you may take the view that certain of the organization's functions are so routine that they are less likely to have unpredictable information needs, or requirements that they can't satisfy from their own internal resources. You might, for example, put the Head of Finance or the Head of Personnel into this category, because they are largely providing routine support services – paying the bills, sending out the invoices, chasing the debts, paying the salaries, sorting out tax and National Insurance. However, you shouldn't rule them out entirely as potential clients. Finance may suddenly come to you for background information on a bad payer. Personnel may have an urgent need for a law report that establishes a precedent in a disciplinary case. But you can probably safely regard these kinds of enquiry as the exception rather than the rule.

Other senior colleagues are much more likely to have regular information needs that they can't easily satisfy internally. These may include the Heads of:

- **Research** – looking for background information on the environment in which the organization is operating, or on social or economic issues that may affect your organization
- **Business Development** – seeking information on new markets or activities into which the organization is considering expanding
- **Competitive Intelligence** – watching out for competitive threats against which the organization needs to protect itself, or opportunities to win business from competitors
- **External Relations** – gathering background information on other bodies with which the organization is considering going into partnership.

These are just a few examples – and, of course, the actual job titles will vary from one organization to another. So you will need to use your experience and, above all, your imagination to work out in advance which are your best targets and what their information needs are likely to be. In fact, you'll be doing exactly the same as you've always done when deciding how to tackle new enquiries – imagining what the final answer will look like.

The meeting

Once you have secured a date and time for your meeting, it's vital not to spoil the opportunity by going to it unprepared. Firstly, you need to know in advance how long it is scheduled to last. This may be your one and only opportunity in a long time to quiz the decision-maker concerned, so you must ensure that you are able to cover your entire agenda in the time available. Fortunately, your enquiry desk experience will help you here too. Remember Kipling's six honest serving men? You can use them to structure your precious meeting time with the decision-makers. Examples of questions you might consider asking include:

- **Who** are you? (You'll know the name and job title of the person you're meeting, of course, but will need to find out about the department they head, including its structure and divisions.)
- **What** does your department do? (This is where you find out in more detail what falls within the department's specific remit – e.g. how do the functions of the Sales Department differ from those of Marketing, or how does the role of the External Relations Department overlap with that of the Overseas Department?)
- **When** do you find that you need information that you can't provide for yourself? (Is there a pattern to the department's year – an especially urgent need for information towards the end of the financial year, or in the run-up to the organization's annual general meeting, for example?)
- **Where** do you get your information from at the moment? (This is your opportunity to find out about the sources and delivery media the department currently uses. Bear in mind that the department might not currently be using the best sources or delivery media for the job. Or you may even discover that most of the information it uses is inside people's heads.)
- **Why** do you need this information? (This is your opportunity to discover more about what the department does, so you can understand the reason behind its information needs.)
- **How** do you manage the information you keep in the department? (This can help you to start considering whether you can meet some of the department's information needs more efficiently than it can itself, thereby reducing its costs and demonstrating your own value to the organization.)

As was the case when you were taking enquiries in your previous job, you wouldn't necessarily ask the questions in this order. The decision-maker will volunteer some of the answers – maybe even most of them – leaving you to ensure that all the ground has been covered and knowing exactly what final issues you still need to address as the meeting comes to a close. And, just as with your previous enquirers, you will encounter decision-makers who are generalists, know-alls, obsessively secretive – even muddlers.

Follow-up: managing initial expectations

It will be extraordinary if you don't come away from at least some of these meetings with an enquiry or two to tackle straight away. In fact, you may find that people are so delighted and relieved that there's an information profes-sional finally in post to help them that they offload months' if not years' worth of accumulated queries onto you, and of course expect an instant solu-tion to their needs. Obviously you're going to have to manage their expectations if you're not to risk your own as yet untried reputation by promising too much too soon. Nevertheless, you will have to provide some-thing as early as possible, and all your previously acquired skills will come into play again.

Firstly, you'll need to work out what is easy and quick to deliver, and what is hard and slow, and prioritize your responses on that basis. Remember, this is so that everyone gets something to read at the earliest possible opportunity. At first, quite a lot of what you're asked for is likely to be hard and slow, because you're still learning about the specialism in which your new organi-zation operates, and the information sources that serve it. So you'll need to be ready to provide 'quick & dirty' answers (see page 69) in the first instance as an earnest of good faith, and to keep your enquirers informed about progress as you find out more on their behalf.

Secondly, you'll need to start working out whose information needs are vital to the organization, and who is simply making use of you because you're there. When you're starting out in a new job, and eager to please whoever comes along, it's all too easy to become embroiled in the detailed require-ments of people who are frankly more demanding than their importance to the organization merits. There's no easy way of dealing with this once you've been sucked in, so the important thing is to be aware of the risk and learn to recognize it when it comes along. There are some danger signs you can spot: the enquirer who comes back day after day with one little query after another;

the person who tries to butter you up by lavishing far more praise on you than you think your efforts merit; the type who claims that they have been personally asked to look into something by the Chief Executive or Chairman, and implies that heads will roll if their requirements aren't given top priority.

Frequently, a discreet phone call to your favoured mentor within the organization (your line manager, perhaps, or your tame interview panel member) may be sufficient to establish how important the demanding enquirer's needs really are. This can enable you to assign a more appropriate degree of priority to their demands, in the reasonable certainty that you will be backed up if they complain.

Identifying the sources that will meet your users' needs

Dealing with these *ad hoc* enquiries, gathered as a result of your initial meetings with decision-makers, will kickstart your knowledge of the information sources and services appropriate to your organization's specialism. In fact, it will be astonishing if the decision-makers you meet don't mention some of the key sources themselves. This will give you a useful shortlist of sources to investigate, and two types are likely to predominate. Firstly, there will be tried and tested print publications that the department or its head have been using for years – industry directories or buyers' guides, for example. Secondly, there will be websites – probably large numbers of them. Most people in the organization, if not all, are likely to have access to the internet on their desks, so it's pretty much inevitable that they will have used it to try to satisfy for themselves requests for information that will now become your responsibility.

It will certainly be worth following up any and all sources suggested by the people you have met. But don't fall into the trap of assuming that that's all you will need to do in order to provide an effective information service. It's very unlikely that any of these people will have taken an overview of all potentially useful sources, and assessed them in any comprehensive way. It's far more likely that they will be using the publications because they are both available and familiar (irrespective of whether they are the best tools for the job) and that they will have accumulated their clutch of favourite websites through not much more than haphazard browsing and colleagues' recommendations. It will be your job to take a comprehensive view of what's available and to decide what best meets the organization's needs.

The questions you need to ask yourself first

You can't start considering sources, services and delivery media properly until you have a good idea of what your organization needs. Now, after your meetings with key decision-makers, is the time to consider what you have learned about your organization and to discover for yourself what sources will begin to satisfy its needs.

You may be starting from scratch, with nothing but your colleagues' unmet information needs to go on, or you may have inherited a room full of publications – books, reference materials, journals – from a long-departed predecessor. You may also have encountered searching aids – catalogues, information files, resource lists, web links – that your predecessor maintained. Any or all of this may be helpful to you, but you should still go back to basics and ask yourself four fundamental questions:

- What's going on in my organization's specialism now?
- Who are the major players?
- How are they communicating with each other?
- How do I find out about earlier developments?

Finding out what's happening now

To find out what's going on in your organization's specialism now, your best starting point is almost certainly the trade and professional press. You may well find copies of some of the relevant titles in your organization already – either in your own information unit or lying around on colleagues' desks – and you should have discovered from some of the people you've met and interviewed what trade magazines and professional journals they read regularly. In addition, *Benn's Media*, *Willing's Press Guide* and *Ulrich's International Periodicals Directory* (in their print or online forms) will help you confirm that you haven't missed any important titles. *Benn's* and *Willing's* are direct competitors, so you won't need to check both; either will do. They cover trade, professional and general periodicals worldwide (although remember that no one source is truly comprehensive in its coverage). *Ulrich's* is slightly different; it concentrates on the heavier professional and academic journals worldwide rather than the lighter trade press.

Having decided which trade and professional journals you need to consider, you don't necessarily have to commit yourself to subscribing to them straight away. Your chosen titles will almost certainly have websites, where you may be able to see sample content from recent editions. Or you can contact the publishers for a sample printed copy.

The trade and professional press is only the starting point for finding out what's happening now. In addition there will be discussion lists, blogs, news websites (maybe with RSS feeds; see page 106) that you will also need to consider. But the traditional trade and professional press is an excellent key to unlock all these other resources. (We'll return to ways in which you can exploit the trade and professional press later.)

Identifying the major players

The trade and professional press will also start giving you clues as to who are the major players in your organization's specialism. They will be the organizations and individuals whose names keep coming up on the news pages, in RSS feeds and in blogs. To make contact with them, and to find out more about what they do and how they're structured, you'll also need to know about the directories that are published in your specialism. As with the press, there are directories in every imaginable specialism, available in both print and electronic form. It's almost inconceivable that there won't be at least one or two that will prove useful to your organization. So check *Current British Directories* for the UK ones – or *Ulrich's Periodicals Directory*, which covers directories internationally as well as journals.

Directory publishers are less likely than the press to let you have sample printed copies on approval, but they will almost certainly have websites (whose addresses you will find in *Current British Directories* and *Ulrich's*) where you will be able to get a good feel for their publications' content and coverage. You may even be able to interrogate some of the sources as well, on a pay-as-you-go basis, before deciding whether or not to subscribe.

The other type of major player to consider in your field is the professional and trade associations that regulate your organization's specialism and act as a forum for its members. *Directory of British Associations* and numerous international equivalents will give you brief details of the associations you need to be aware of. Incidentally, these sources will also give you the associations' web addresses; professionally edited and quality controlled, they are a much more reliable way of finding the associations you need on the web than simply using a generic web search engine.

Discovering how these players are communicating with one another

Even though they may be in competition – for customers if they are profit-seeking organizations, for members or funding if not-for-profit – the players in your organization's specialist field will also be communicating with each other in a myriad different ways. Their representatives will be attending conferences and giving papers, debating hot topics on discussion lists, writing to the trade and professional press, entering into partnerships or consortia for mutual benefit, jointly publishing reports. It's going to be a challenge for you to keep up with this huge volume of activity; you'll almost certainly have to be selective in what you monitor.

If you do have to pick just one way of monitoring all this communication, then, again, the basic trade press is probably the best single source. It's the job of trade journalists not only to know what's going on but also to know what's important for your specialism – and at the same time, press offices and public relations firms representing all your specialism's players will be feeding those journalists with news items for their consideration. Many of the news stories and articles that the trade magazines cover will refer to conference papers or new reports – frequently even including a web address from which you can download individual papers or at least executive summaries of them.

You can wait for the next printed issue of your chosen trade journal or journals to come out if you wish. Or, increasingly, you can take an RSS feed, with news items delivered to you online as they break – frequently in advance of their publication in the printed journal. (We'll return to the question of exploiting your information sources shortly.)

Finding out about earlier developments

The sources and strategies we've considered already will help you keep up-to-date with what's going on now. But you will need to consider yet further sources for searching the archives of your specialism's accumulated knowledge down the years. As with the trade press and directories, there are innumerable searchable archives of professional and academic journals, conference papers and reports. Some are owned by large scale academic and professional journal publishers, and feature only titles from their own publishing stable. Others are created by specialist bodies in the field – research institutes, professional associations, academic faculties or consortia, and commercial publishers. You'll need to find out which ones you should consider providing to your users.

The comprehensively useful *Know It All, Find It Fast* will alert you to the existence of many of these archive databases (and will give you web addresses so that you will be able to follow up the details of individual services for yourself). However, you will find much more in-depth coverage of these and other high-quality resources over the coming years in the volumes of *The New Walford: Guide to Reference Resources*. Only the first volume of this comprehensive three-volume bibliography has been published at the time of writing – covering science, technology & medicine. The other two volumes – dealing with social sciences & the arts, and with humanities & general reference respectively – will appear over the next couple of years.

Customer needs first – sources second

With all the demands for information that you are likely to be faced with from day one, it would be tempting to start acquiring sources straight away. Resist the temptation if you can. You really do need to be sure that you're buying the most cost-effective sources and services for your organization, in the most appropriate delivery media. So do try to have those meetings with key decision-makers first. As soon as they know you're in the market – because you've asked for a sample copy of the trade magazine, for example – publishers will start bombarding you with flyers and offers. By the time that starts happening, you need to be sure that you really do understand what sources would most benefit the organization, so that you're not swayed by publishers' blandishments.

All the same, you shouldn't dismiss all this promotional literature as junk mail. It's actually likely to be pretty well targeted to your requirements. So give each piece of mail just a few seconds' consideration before you consign it to the waste paper basket; every so often, your hand will be stayed because you've spotted something potentially useful. The important thing to remember, though, is that your stock and selection policies should be driven by your organization's needs – and you have to know what those needs are before you can start acquiring sources with confidence.

Exploiting your sources

Once you've invested in all those sources, should you just let them lie fallow and wait for people to come along and discover them? Absolutely not! Once the initial flurry of interest in the arrival of an information professional in the organization has died down, you'll need to constantly refresh your users' interest in your service. Without too much difficulty, you can use your newly acquired sources and services both to promote your information service, and to add to its resources.

The trade media

Once again, there's no better place to start exploiting your service than with the trade press – or the trade media as we shall now call it, since you can make use of it in all its delivery forms – weekly or monthly magazine, RSS feed, blog, discussion list or searchable archive.

Let's start with the printed publication. If it's typical of the usual format, it will have news stories (probably written by staff journalists), feature articles (some by journalists, some by guest writers), regular opinion pieces (probably by specialists in the subject who have a flair for writing provocatively), book and product reviews (contributed by specialists as a rule), possibly an irreverent end piece, and masses of ads, both display and classified. You can make use of all of these sections.

Take a look at the news stories. See how many of them are based on other literature – newly published reports or surveys, for example. The news story will usually tell you where you can get hold of these reports as well, giving you an address, a phone number, an e-mail address or a website. You might then decide to buy the paper report, or you may simply provide a link to it on your own organization's intranet. Either way, you've added both to your stock and to the value of your information service.

A glance at the articles and opinion pieces will tell you what the hot issues are at the moment, and who's talking about them. So, when a senior manager or – worse – his dragon of a PA phones up and barks a request for information on a new topic, you will at least recognize the buzzwords used and recall that you have seen something about it. That should be sufficient to enable you to go back to the paper's website and seek out the article in the charged-for, password-protected area of the site.

The reviews can help you identify core literature in your organization's specialism – new editions of standard textbooks, for example – that you may need to acquire to bolster your core collection. The display ads are your guide to sources and services that support your organization's specialism, and the classifieds are your up-to-date buyer's guide.

So, do get into the habit of giving each issue of a title a few minutes' attention when it first comes in. Just ten minutes skimming through can be a really worthwhile investment of your time.

Professional and academic journals

Professional and academic journals are a different kind of beast from the weekly or monthly trade magazines. Sober and restrained in appearance, they're likely to contain a comparatively small number of lengthy articles, written by specialists in the field and including plenty of supporting detail and references to further literature on the subject. Many of the articles may well be worth cataloguing and indexing as separate information sources in their own right, of particular value to your organization. The lists of references included with particularly pertinent articles may lead you to further publications that you need to acquire to further enhance your core collection. And review articles can help you bolster your core collection of books and reports.

Another particularly effective way of exploiting professional and academic journals is to alert your organization to their contents. You can do this quite simply – by creating a classified list of the articles in a newly received journal and e-mailing it round the organization or to selected users, or by posting the information on your intranet.

RSS feeds, blogs, discussion lists

Valuable as all your printed sources are, they're only the beginning. RSS feeds, blogs and discussion lists can all add to the information resources you can deliver to your organization, and raise the profile of your service at the same time. So what do they do, how can you identify them and how can you decide what to use?

RSS feeds provide an easy way for you to be up-to-date with the websites you want to keep track of regularly. Instead of having to visit them to see if they've added a new page, you can use RSS (which is short for Really Simple Syndication) to be informed automatically whenever they add something new. To run RSS, you first need to download a program called a news reader. This displays your chosen RSS news feeds on your screen. After you've installed the software, you then choose which RSS feeds you want, following the instructions for your particular news reader to add new sites to your list of chosen feeds. (Usually this is as simple as copying the address of the feed and pasting it into the reader.) More and more specialist websites are adding RSS facilities, so you may well find that your most useful trade magazine or blog sites are available to you in this way. There is a variety of different news readers available for PCs and Macs – some free, some charged-for. You can find links to a good selection of them at the RSS Specifications site (www.rss-specifications.com).

Blogs (short for weblogs) have already come up in Chapter 5. They are personal online diaries published on the web. There are thousands and thousands of them and their numbers are growing fast, so you will need to be very selective in the ones you choose to follow. If you want to keep track of information in your field using this medium, why not start, once again, with your trusty trade and professional magazines? Expert columnists who write regularly for these publications may well have their own blogs, which they will very likely promote in their columns, so this could be a useful way of identifying blogs that will genuinely have something valuable to say. Blogs frequently incorporate RSS feeds as well, so you don't even need to visit them regularly in order to keep up with them. As with RSS feeds, the danger with blogs is that you will be tempted to take so much information by this medium that you rapidly have more than you can cope with. So, instead of taking them for yourself, you could simply keep track of what's available, provide links to them on your intranet, and alert your users to feeds or blogs that you think they might be interested in taking for themselves.

Discussion lists are online forums to which a community of people contributes. The messages from each contributor are frequently organized as navigable discussion 'threads' on particular topics, accessible via a website. Individual contributions (or 'postings') are also delivered to all the list members by e-mail, either as soon as they are posted or else in batches at regular intervals. Discussion lists may be closed – accessible by a particular group of people only – or open – available to anyone who wants to register to use them. Some discussion lists are moderated, which means that there is someone with an editorial role ensuring, for example, that lists don't get overloaded with trivia or repetition, and that contributors treat each other courteously. Others are not, and can become so anarchic and acrimonious as to be well nigh useless as a serious information source. Again, you may want to keep yourself aware of relevant discussion lists, and post links to them on your intranet so that your users can join them if they wish.

Promoting your service

Whatever kind of information service you provide, you must never make the mistake of sitting back and waiting for people to visit it. This matters if your organization operates out of one site and all your users are in the same building – but it matters even more if they are scattered throughout the country or even the world, and communicate mostly by intranet, e-mail and phone. We've already seen how you need to start by getting to know your users and their needs, and to segment them to ensure that the right services go to the right people. To protect your service, and ensure that it has the resources to develop when opportunity arises, you must also keep your profile high.

So consider inventing a special name for your service. Develop a corporate identity for it, based on your organization's logo, and add a strapline drawing attention to the value you can add. Keep your service in the public eye by regularly telling your users what's new – and concentrate on the benefits that your new services deliver, not on the sources you have acquired. Encourage your best initial users to become advocates and champions for your service, recommending it to other decision-makers who might not have been prepared to talk to you the first time you approached them. And when pitching to any potential new user, concentrate on their needs, not on your sources.

You also need to lock your users in by constantly feeding them fresh information – through a current awareness or selective dissemination of information (SDI) service for example, based on material you find in the trade or professional media. Your users will probably be able to access directly over the web many of the new services you tell them about; so regard this as an opportunity to free up your time for fresh developments, rather than as a threat to you as the organization's information provider. If you help your users to become self-sufficient in answering routine enquiries, and concentrate on the difficult ones yourself, that can only enhance your reputation, not diminish it.

Getting help and support

Running a small information unit can be a lonely and isolating experience – especially if you're the only information professional in the organization. You'll need help and support – practical and moral – from time to time. And you'll certainly need advice on how you can do your job better. Fortunately, this is a very supportive profession, and there's no shortage of places you can turn to for help.

Fellow information workers

Although you may feel isolated, you certainly won't be alone. There will be fellow information professionals working in other organizations in your field, whose brains you can pick for ideas to develop your service further. You may be able to identify some of them through the directories relating to your organization's specialism that you will have acquired by now. Alternatively, there are several specialist information profession directories that can help you. Try the *Aslib Directory of Information Sources in the United Kingdom*, for example, or take a look at the *Directory of British Associations* (or its numerous international equivalents) to see if any of the associations in your field has a library or information unit where there might be specialist information professionals willing to lend a listening ear.

This won't be a one-way process, of course; you must expect to have your brains picked in return. You'll also need to bear in mind that your supportive fellow information professional may well be working for one of your competitors. However this shouldn't prevent you from making contact; you both just need to ensure that you restrict your discussions to matters of professional practice, and don't risk giving away confidential information about your organization's activities.

Professional associations

You can get plenty of further support from your professional peers by joining some of the multiplicity of membership organizations and special interest groups that the library and information profession spawns. Going to meetings of professional groups may prove less hazardous than meeting fellow professionals informally on a one-to-one basis. Group meetings are more likely to be held on neutral territory and to be more public affairs, so there's less likelihood of participants laying themselves open to possible accusations of collusion with competitors. Bigger associations such as CILIP: the Chartered Institute of Library and Information Professionals (www.cilip.org.uk), the Special Libraries Association (www.sla.org) and Aslib (www.aslib.com) each have their own special interest groups. There are also plenty of smaller but no less lively independent associations – for law librarians, media information professionals or people providing information to the financial services sector, for example. The *Directory of British Associations* or their international equivalents will enable you to identify some of the other specialist associations in the library and information field.

Online discussion lists

If you can't easily get to meetings of special interest groups, then you may well be able to participate virtually by joining an online discussion list. Once again, their numbers are legion and there can be few professional groups in the information field that don't offer some kind of online discussion facility. Just like the people who contribute to them, discussion lists tend to have good days and bad days. Sometimes you'll encounter really useful discussions about information sources that can help with a particularly difficult enquiry. At other times the same discussion lists seem to be offering nothing but gripes. One honourable exception to this rule is FreePint (www.freepint.com). It is a huge international community of information professionals, predominantly working in special libraries and information services, who between them help people find the best information sources for particularly difficult enquiries, as well as offering ideas for solving hardware and software problems, and discussing career issues. But it's far more than just a discussion list; it also has a regular free online newsletter, including a section where practising information professionals review favourite websites in their particular field.

Training and publications

As you develop your information service, there will be plenty of other things you'll need to know that are outside the scope of this book. You may need to learn the basics of cataloguing and classification (or metadata and taxonomies if you prefer), so that you can manage your collection efficiently and make it accessible to your users. You may decide to use a generic database package for this purpose, such as Microsoft Access, and be looking for a refresher in using it effectively. You'll need to find out about interlibrary loan and document delivery services, and about copyright and licensing, to ensure that your copying and downloading don't infringe intellectual property rights. You'll want to buy equipment and software – something as basic as shelving and furniture, or as sophisticated as RFID self-issuing software or a networked enquiry management system, for example. For all of these needs and more, help is at hand in the form of training and practical guides.

Several library and information organizations offer a comprehensive range of short one- and two-day courses in every aspect of running an information service, so check out Aslib (www.aslib.com), CILIP (www.cilip.org.uk) and TFPL (www.tfpl.com) to see what's available from them. Facet Publishing (owned by CILIP) publishes scores of practical handbooks just like this one on enquiry handling, covering other topics that we haven't been able to touch on here, so take a look at their online catalogue at www.facetpublishing.co.uk. If you are setting up your own service, for instance, you can get masses of further help from Facet's *Setting Up a Library and Information Service From Scratch* by Sheila Pantry and Peter Griffiths. And when it comes to sourcing the equipment and services you need, both CILIP and *Information World Review* (www.iwr.co.uk) publish buyers' guides, and there are plenty of ads, too, in *Information World Review*, in *Managing Information* from Aslib, and in CILIP's members-only magazine *Library & Information Gazette*.

Your goal: successful enquiry answering – every time

So that's it! With a little care and common sense – plus a lively and imaginative approach – you can make enquiry answering one of the most satisfying and fulfilling work activities there is. The explosion of available information, the technological developments that can help you retrieve and enhance it, and the enormously increased public awareness of the value of information – all combine to make the prospects for library and information professionals more exciting than ever before. What you need to do is to grasp those opportunities. So the only thing that remains to be done now is to wish you success with your enquiry answering – every time.

To recap . . .

■ **Start by finding out what your users need – then make sure that your information resources will meet those needs.**

■ **Use your sources to find out what's going on in your organization's specialism now, who the major players are, and how they are communicating with each other.**

■ **Exploit your information sources to raise the profile of your service**

■ **Don't be afraid to look for professional help and support.**

Guide to key reference sources

Full details of key sources mentioned in the book, with annotations

Full details of all the 25 multi-purpose reference sources listed on pages xviii–xx, and their international equivalents, appear here. You'll find them useful for getting started on a wide range of enquiries.

Most of these sources started as print publications; only those with editions published in 2000 or later are included here. However, many are now available online as well, and some may also offer CD-ROM versions. Some are online only. This situation is changing all the time as publishers adapt their titles and content to reflect the requirements of customers and the capabilities of electronic media.

The information for this guide has been taken from publishers' websites, with full contact details given wherever possible, and telephone numbers shown with their international country code. When investigating any of these sources, or confirming contact details, I strongly recommend that you visit the publisher's website first, to make sure that you have access to the most up-to-date information available.

Abstracts in New Technologies and Engineering
Subject index (with brief abstracts from 1993) to articles in UK and US science and technology journals. Available in print and online.
Companion sources: *British Humanities Index, Applied Social Sciences Index and Abstracts, Sociological Abstracts.*
Comparable sources: *Applied Science and Technology Index/Abstracts/full text, General Science Index/Abstracts/full text.*
CSA, 4640 Kingsgate, Cascade Way, Oxford Business Park South, Oxford, OX4 2ST. Tel: +44 (0)1865 336250. Fax: +44 (0)1865 336258. E-mail: eurosales@csa.com. Web: www.csa.com.

Amazon.com
Online general store specializing in sale of current and out of print books, its features including search facility, reader reviews and suggestions for related titles. Web: www.amazon.com.

Annual Abstract of Statistics
Comprehensive collection of statistics on all subjects, usually abstracted from more detailed government statistical publications. Statistics also available online at www.statistics.gov.uk.
Complementary sources: *Europe in Figures: Eurostat Yearbook, United Nations Statistical Yearbook.*
Office for National Statistics. Available through TSO Orders/Post Cash Dept, PO Box 29, Norwich NR3 1GN. Tel: +44 (0)870 600 5522. Fax: +44 (0)870 600 5533. E-mail: customer.services@tso.co.uk. Web: www.tso.co.uk.

Annual Register
Provides details of the year's events on a country-by-country basis, plus a political, social and economic overview of each country.
Comparable sources: *Europa World Yearbook, Statesman's Yearbook, World Factbook.*
Keesing's Worldwide, 28a Hills Road, Cambridge CB2 1LA. Tel: +44 (0)1223 508050. Fax: +44 (0)1223 508049. E-mail: info@keesings.com. Web: www.keesings.com.

Applied Science and Technology Index/Abstracts/full text
Subject index, with abstracts and latterly full text, to articles in English language science and technology journals published worldwide. Available in print, on CD-ROM and online.
Companion sources: *General Science Index/Abstracts/full text, Humanities Index/Abstracts/full text, Social Sciences Index/Abstracts/full text,* Wilson OmniFile Full Text Mega Edition.
Comparable source: *Abstracts in New Technologies and Engineering.*
H W Wilson Co, 950 University Avenue, Bronx, New York 10452. Tel: +001 718 588 8400. Fax: +001 718 590 1617. E-mail: custserv@hwwilson.com. Web: www.hwwilson.com.
UK & European agent: Thompson Henry Ltd, London Road, Sunningdale, Berks SL5 0EP. Tel: +44 (0)1344 624615. Fax: +44 (0)1344 626120. E-mail: s.piddington@thompsonhenry.co.uk. Web: www.thompsonhenry.co.uk.

Applied Social Sciences Index and Abstracts
Subject index, with abstracts, to articles mostly in United Kingdom social science journals. Available in print and online.
Companion sources: *Abstracts in New Technologies and Engineering, British Humanities Index, Sociological Abstracts.*
Comparable source: *Social Sciences Index/Abstracts/full text.*
CSA, 4640 Kingsgate, Cascade Way, Oxford Business Park South, Oxford, OX4 2ST. Tel: +44 (0)1865 336250. Fax: +44 (0)1865 336258. E-mail: eurosales@csa.com. Web: www.csa.com.

Aslib Directory of Information Sources in the United Kingdom
Gives details of services available from special libraries and information units, including terms and conditions for access.
Aslib Books & Directories, Aslib/Routledge Reference, Taylor & Francis Group Ltd, 2 Park Square, Milton Park, Abingdon, Oxford OX14 4RN. Tel: + 44 (0)20 7842 2133. Fax: + 44 (0)20 7842 2249. E-mail: info.europa@ tandf.co.uk. Web: www. europapublications. co.uk.

BBC News Online
Comprehensive general news service updated throughout the day with a fully searchable archive.
Comparable service: *Keesing's Record of World Events.*
Web: http://news.bbc.co.uk.

Benn's Media
Gives full publication details of newspapers and journals by subject.
Competitor: *Willing's Press Guide.*
Comparable source: *Ulrich's Periodicals Directory.*
Annual. 3 vols: United Kingdom, Europe, World.
CMP Information Ltd, Sovereign House, Sovereign Way, Tonbridge, Kent, TN9 1RW. Tel: +44 (0)1732 377591. Fax: +44 (0)1732 367301. E-mail: bennsmedia@cmpinformation.com. Web: www.cmpdata.com.

British Humanities Index
Subject index (with abstracts from 1991) to articles in British and other English language humanities journals. Available in print and online.
Companion sources: *Abstracts in New Technologies and Engineering, Applied Social Sciences Index and Abstracts, Sociological Abstracts.*

Comparable source: *Humanities Index/Abstracts/full text.*
CSA, 4640 Kingsgate, Cascade Way, Oxford Business Park South, Oxford, OX4 2ST. Tel: +44 (0)1865 336250. Fax: +44 (0)1865 336258. E-mail: eurosales@csa.com. Web: www.csa.com.

British Library Direct
British Library Inside
Online services that allows you to search for millions of journal articles and conference papers, either by title or subject, and order them online.
Comparable services: Emerald Insight, Ingenta Connect, Sage Full Text Collections, Wilson Omni File Full Text Mega Edition.
Web: http://direct.bl.uk, www.bl.uk/services/current/inside.html.

British Library Integrated Catalogue
Includes entries for millions of items available from the British Library, either for reference, loan or supply as photocopies. Also provides links to other BL resources and leading UK and overseas library catalogues.
Comparable services: *British National Bibliography, Global Books in Print,* LibWeb.
Web: http://catalogue.bl.uk.

British National Bibliography
Gives details of all books and pamphlets placed on legal deposit in the British Library, classified by subject. Available in print and on CD-ROM.
Comparable services: British Library Integrated Catalogue, *Global Books in Print,* LibWeb.
British Library, Bibliographic Standards and Systems, Boston Spa, Wetherby, West Yorkshire LS23 7BQ. Tel: +44 (0)1937 546585. Fax: +44 (0)1937 546586. E-mail: bss-info@bl.uk. Web: www.bl.uk.

Centres, Bureaux and Research Institutes
Gives details of centres of expertise in a wide range of fields.
Councils, Committees and Boards including Government Agencies and Authorities
Gives details of official and public bodies and quangos in the United Kingdom.
Current British Directories
Describes contents of directories and reference works published in the UK.

Comparable source: *Ulrich's Periodicals Directory.*

Companion sources to all: *Directory of British Associations and Associations in Ireland, Directory of European Professional and Learned Societies.*

CBD Research Ltd, 15 Wickham Road, Beckenham, Kent BR3 2JS. Tel: +44 (0)20 8650 7745. Fax: +44 (0)20 8650 0768. E-mail: cbd@cbdresearch.com. Web: www.cbdresearch.com.

Dialog
Dialog DataStar

Multipurpose online archives permitting sophisticated searching of thousands of sources with global coverage on all subjects.

Comparable services: LexisNexis.

Web: www.dialog.com.

Directory of British Associations and Associations in Ireland
Directory of European Professional and Learned Societies

Uniform series giving details of associations, societies and other organizations throughout the UK and Europe respectively. *Directory of British Associations* also available on CD-ROM.

Companion sources: *Centres, Bureaux and Research Institutes, Councils, Committees and Boards, Current British Directories.*

Comparable sources: *Encyclopaedia of Associations: International Organizations, Europa Directory of International Organizations, World Directory of Trade and Business Associations, Yearbook of International Organizations.*

CBD Research Ltd, 15 Wickham Road, Beckenham, Kent BR3 2JS. Tel: +44 (0)20 8650 7745. Fax: +44 (0)20 8650 0768. E-mail: cbd@cbdresearch.com. Web: www.cbdresearch.com.

Emerald Insight

Online service providing searchable abstracts and full text of management, science & technology and library and information journal articles.

Comparable services: British Library Direct, British Library Inside, Ingenta Connect, Sage Full Text Collections, Wilson OmniFile Full Text Mega Edition.

Web: www.emeraldinsight.com.

Encyclopaedia of Associations: International Organizations
Gives details of professional and trade associations, societies and institutions in the United States and internationally. Available online and on CD-ROM as *Associations Unlimited.*
Competitors: *Europa Directory of International Organizations, Yearbook of International Organizations.*
Comparable source: *World Directory of Trade and Business Associations.*
Thomson Learning Library Reference EMEA, High Holborn House, 50–51 Bedford Row, London WC1R 4LR. Tel: +44 (0)20 7607 2500. Fax: +44 (0)20 7067 2600. E-mail: enquiries@thomson.com. Web: www.gale.com.

Europa Directory of International Organizations
Gives details of international and world regional organizations.
Competitors: *Encyclopaedia of Associations: International Organizations, Yearbook of International Organizations.*
Comparable source: *World Directory of Trade and Business Associations.*
Companion sources: *Europa World of Learning, Europa World Yearbook.*

Europa World of Learning
Gives details of universities, colleges, learned societies, research institutes and museums worldwide. Also available online at www.worldoflearning. com.
Companion sources: *Europa Directory of International Organizations, Europa World Yearbook.*

Europa World Yearbook
Describes the political, social and economic life of each country of the world, with details of main institutions.
Comparable sources: *Annual Register, Statesman's Yearbook, World Factbook.*
Complementary source: *UK . . . the Official Yearbook of the United Kingdom of Great Britain and Northern Ireland.*
Companion sources: *Europa Directory of International Organizations, Europa World of Learning.*
Routledge Reference, Taylor & Francis Group Ltd, 2 Park Square, Milton Park, Abingdon, Oxford OX14 4RN. Tel: + 44 (0)20 7842 2133. Fax: + 44 (0)20 7842 2249. E-mail: info.europa@tandf.co.uk. Web: www. europapublications. co.uk.

Europe in Figures: Eurostat Yearbook

Comprehensive collection of statistics on all subjects, comparing European Union member states and usually abstracted from more detailed Eurostat publications.

Complementary sources: *Annual Abstract of Statistics, United Nations Statistical Yearbook.*

Office for National Statistics. Available (for Eurostat) through TSO Orders/Post Cash Dept, PO Box 29, Norwich NR3 1GN. Tel: +44 (0)870 600 5522. Fax: +44 (0)870 600 5533. E-mail: customer.services@tso.co.uk. (Equivalent agents operate in other European Union member states as well; see Eurostat website for details.) Web: www.tso.co.uk. Eurostat web: http://epp.eurostat.cec.eu.int.

General Science Index/Abstracts/full text

Subject index, with abstracts and some full text, to articles in English language science journals published worldwide. Available in print, on CD-ROM and online.

Companion sources: *Applied Science and Technology Index/Abstracts/ full text, Humanities Index/Abstracts/full text, Social Sciences Index/ Abstracts/full text*, Wilson OmniFile Full Text Mega Edition.

Comparable source: *Abstracts in New Technologies and Engineering.*

H W Wilson Co, 950 University Avenue, Bronx, New York 10452. Tel: +001 718 588 8400. Fax: +001 718 590 1617. E-mail: custserv@hwwilson.com. Web: www.hwwilson.com.

UK & European agent: Thompson Henry Ltd, London Road, Sunningdale, Berks SL5 0EP. Tel: +44 (0)1344 624615. Fax: +44 (0)1344 626120. E-mail: s.piddington@thompsonhenry.co.uk. Web: www.thompsonhenry.co.uk.

Global Books in Print

Gives bibliographic details of currently available English language books worldwide. Available on CD-ROM and online as www.globalbooksinprint. com.

Comparable services: British Library Integrated Catalogue, *British National Bibliography*, LibWeb.

Bowker UK & International Ltd, Farringdon House, 3rd Floor, Wood Street, East Grinstead, West Sussex RH19 1UZ. Tel: +44 (0)1342 310450 Fax: +44 (0)1342 310486. E-mail: sales@bowker.co.uk. Web: www.bowker.co.uk.

Google Books Library Project
Developing online service providing searchable digitized images of books in major research libraries, initially in the United States and the UK. Web: http://books.google.com.

Hollis UK Public Relations Annual
Hollis Europe
Companion volumes giving details of public relations departments and press offices of a very large number of organizations. Also available online. Hollis Directories Ltd, Harlequin House, 7 High Street, Teddington, Middlesex TW11 8EL. Tel: +44 (0)20 8977 7711. Fax: +44 (0)20 8977 1133. E-mail: orders@hollis-pr.co.uk. Web: www.hollis-pr.com.

Humanities Index/Abstracts/full text
Subject index, latterly with abstracts and full text, to articles in English language humanities journals published worldwide. Available in different versions in print, on CD-ROM and online.
Companion sources: *Applied Science and Technology Index/Abstracts/full text, General Science Index/Abstracts/full text, Social Sciences Index/ Abstracts/full text*, Wilson OmniFile Full Text Mega Edition.
Comparable source: *British Humanities Index*.
H W Wilson Co, 950 University Avenue, Bronx, New York 10452. Tel: +001 718 588 8400. Fax: +001 718 590 1617. E-mail: custserv@ hwwilson.com. Web: www.hwwilson.com.
UK & European agent: Thompson Henry Ltd, London Road, Sunningdale, Berks SL5 0EP. Tel: +44 (0)1344 624615. Fax: +44 (0)1344 626120. E-mail: s.piddington@thompsonhenry.co.uk. Web: www.thompsonhenry.co.uk.

IngentaConnect
Online service providing full text of articles from a large number of academic and professional journals.
Comparable services: British Library Direct, British Library Inside, Emerald Insight, Sage Full Text Collections, Wilson Omnifile Full Text Mega Edition.
Web: www.ingentaconnect.com.

Keesing's Record of World Events
Provides summaries of news from around the world, with regularly updated subject indexes. Available in print, on CD-ROM and online.
Comparable service: BBC News Online.
Keesing's Worldwide, 28a Hills Road, Cambridge CB2 1LA. Tel: +44 (0)1223 508050. Fax: +44 (0)1223 508049. E-mail: info@keesings.com. Web: www.keesings.com.

Know It All, Find It Fast: an A-Z source guide for the enquiry desk
Arranged by subject, suggests a wide range of sources, both printed and electronic, that will help answer some of the commonest enquiries. By Bob Duckett, Peter Walker and Christinea Donnelly.
Companion source: *The New Walford: Guide to Reference Resources.*
Facet Publishing, 7 Ridgmount Street, London WC1E 7AE. Tel: +44 (0)20 7255 0594. Fax: +44 (0)20 7255 0591. E-mail: info@facetpublishing.co.uk. Web: www.facetpublishing.co.uk.

LexisNexis
Multipurpose online archive permitting sophisticated searching of newspaper and journal articles and legal information sources; still significant US focus and emphasis on business, management and law, but other coverage improving.
Comparable services: Dialog, Dialog DataStar.
Web: www.lexisnexis.com.

LibWeb
Online service from Nielsen BookData giving details of current and out-of-print UK, European, United States and South African books.
Comparable services: British Library Integrated Catalogue, *British National Bibliography, Global Books in Print.*
Web: www.nielsenbookdata.co.uk.

The New Walford: Guide to Reference Resources
Comprehensive bibliography of reference material, covering sourcebooks, directories & yearbooks, journals, statistics, online resources and selected textbooks. 3 vols: Science, technology & medicine published 2005; Social sciences due 2006; Humanities & general reference due 2007.

Companion source: *Know It All, Find It Fast: an A-Z source guide for the enquiry desk.*
Facet Publishing, 7 Ridgmount Street, London WC1E 7AE. Tel: +44 (0)20 7255 0594. Fax: +44 (0)20 7255 0591. E-mail: info@facetpublishing.co.uk. Web: www.facetpublishing.co.uk.

Office for National Statistics
Provides large number of UK statistics online, plus guidance on the full range of official statistics available elsewhere as well.
Comparable service: United Nations Statistics Division.
Web: www.statistics.gov.uk.

Sage Full Text Collections
Online service providing full text of journal articles from a wide range of social and scientific journals.
Comparable services: British Library Direct, British Library Inside, Emerald Insight, IngentaConnect, Wilson OmniFile Full Text Mega Edition.
Available online through CSA, 4640 Kingsgate, Cascade Way, Oxford Business Park South, Oxford OX4 2ST. Tel: +44 (0)1865 336250. Fax: +44 (0)1865 336258. E-mail: eurosales@csa.com. Web: www.csa.com.

Setting Up a Library and Information Service from Scratch: Everything you need to know about setting up a library and information service. By Sheila Pantry and Peter Griffiths.
Facet Publishing, 7 Ridgmount Street, London WC1E 7AE. Tel: +44 (0)20 7255 0594. Fax: +44 (0)20 7255 0591. E-mail: info@facetpublishing.co.uk. Web: www.facetpublishing.co.uk.

Social Sciences Index/Abstracts/full text
Subject index, latterly with abstracts and full text, to articles in English language social science journals published worldwide. Available in print, on CD-ROM and online.
Companion sources: *Applied Science and Technology Index/Abstracts/full text, General Science Index/Abstracts/full text, Humanities Index/Abstracts/full text*, Wilson OmniFile Full Text Mega Edition.
Comparable sources: *Applied Social Sciences Index and Abstracts, Sociological Abstracts.*

H W Wilson Co, 950 University Avenue, Bronx, New York 10452. Tel: +001 718 588 8400. Fax: +001 718 590 1617. E-mail: custserv@ hwwilson.com. Web: www.hwwilson.com.

UK & European agent: Thompson Henry Ltd, London Road, Sunningdale, Berks SL5 0EP. Tel: +44 (0)1344 624615. Fax: +44 (0)1344 626120. E-mail: s.piddington@thompsonhenry.co.uk. Web: www.thompsonhenry.co.uk.

Sociological Abstracts

Subject index, with abstracts, to articles, books, chapters and conference papers internationally on the social and behavioural sciences. Available in print and online.

Companion sources: *Abstracts in New Technologies and Engineering, Applied Social Sciences Index and Abstracts, British Humanities Index.*

Comparable source: *Social Sciences Index/Abstracts/full text.*

CSA, 4640 Kingsgate, Cascade Way, Oxford Business Park South, Oxford, OX4 2ST. Tel: +44 (0)1865 336250. Fax: +44 (0)1865 336258. E-mail: eurosales@csa.com. Web: www.csa.com.

Sources of Non-Official UK Statistics

Gives details of non-governmental statistical sources, mostly relating to business and industry. Edited by David Mort.

Complementary source: *World Directory of Non-Official Statistical Sources.*

Gower Publishing Ltd, Gower House, Croft Road, Aldershot, Hants GU11 3HR. Tel: +44 (0)1252 331551. Fax: +44 (0)1252 344405. E-mail: info@gowerpub.com. Web: www.gowerpub.com.

Statesman's Yearbook

Describes the political, social and economic life of each country of the world, with details of main institutions.

Comparable sources: *Annual Register, Europa World Yearbook, World Factbook.*

Complementary source: *UK . . . the Official Yearbook of the United Kingdom of Great Britain and Northern Ireland.*

Palgrave Macmillan Ltd, Houndmills, Basingstoke, Hampshire RG21 6XS. Tel: +44 (0)1256 329242. Fax: +44 (0)1256 479476. E-mail: bookenquiries@palgrave.com. Web: www.palgrave.com.

UK . . .the Official Yearbook of the United Kingdom of Great Britain and Northern Ireland
Describes British political, social and economic life and gives details of principal United Kingdom institutions.
Complementary sources: *Europa World Yearbook, Statesman's Yearbook*.
Office for National Statistics. Available through TSO Orders/Post Cash Dept, PO Box 29, Norwich NR3 1GN. Tel: +44 (0)870 600 5522. Fax: +44 (0)870 600 5533. E-mail: customer.services@tso.co.uk. Web: www.tso.co.uk.

Ulrich's Periodicals Directory
Gives details of major journals, directories and yearbooks published world-wide by subject. Also available on disc and online at www.ulrichsweb.com.
Comparable sources: *Benn's Media, Current British Directories, Willing's Press Guide*.
Bowker UK & International Ltd, Farringdon House, 3rd Floor, Wood Street, East Grinstead, West Sussex RH19 1UZ. Tel: +44 (0)1342 310450 Fax: +44 (0)1342 310486. E-mail: sales@bowker.co.uk. Web: www.bowker.co.uk.

United Nations Statistics Division
Provides online a range of international comparative statistical data on a wide variety of topics.
Comparable service: National Statistics.
Web: http://unstats.un.org/ unsd.
United Nations Statistical Yearbook
Comprehensive collection of statistics on all subjects, comparing most countries of the world. Many statistics also available online from the United Nations Statistics Division at http://unstats.un.org/unsd.
Complementary sources: *Annual Abstract of Statistics, Europe in Figures*: *Eurostat Yearbook*.
United National Department of Economic & Social Affairs, Statistics Division. TSO Orders/Post Cash Dept, PO Box 29, Norwich NR3 1GN. Tel: +44 (0)870 600 5522. Fax: +44 (0)870 600 5533. E-mail: customer.services@tso.co.uk. Web: www.tso.co.uk.

Whitaker's Almanac
Comprehensive repository of brief information on all subjects, from a British point of view; a good starting point for information for which there is no obvious specialist source.

A&C Black, 38 Soho Square, London W1D 3HB. Tel: +44 (0)20 7758 0200. E-mail: customerservices@acblack.com. Web: www.acblack.com.

Willing's Press Guide
Gives full publication details of newspapers and journals by subject. 3 vols: UK, Europe & World. Also available online.
Competitor; *Benn's Media.*
Comparable source: *Ulrich's Periodicals Directory.*
Waymaker Ltd, Chess House, 34 Germain Street, Chesham, Bucks HP5 1SJ. Tel: +44 (0)870 736 0010. Fax: +44 (0)870 736 0011 E-mail: enquiries@willingspress.com. Web: www.willingspress.com.

Wilson OmniFile Full Text Mega Edition
Includes subject index entries and, where available, abstracts and full text drawn from the full range of H W Wilson services, including Education Full Text, General Science Full Text, Humanities Full Text, Readers' Guide Full Text, Social Sciences Full Text, Wilson Business Full Text. Available online only.
Comparable services: British Library Direct, British Library Inside, Emerald Insight, IngentaConnect, Sage Full Text Collections.
H W Wilson Co, 950 University Avenue, Bronx, New York 10452. Tel: +001 718 588 8400. Fax: +001 718 590 1617. E-mail: custserv@ hwwilson.com. Web: www.hwwilson.com.
UK & European agent: Thompson Henry Ltd, London Road, Sunningdale, Berks SL5 0EP. Tel: +44 (0)1344 624615. Fax: +44 (0)1344 626120. E-mail: s.piddington@thompsonhenry.co.uk. Web: www.thompsonhenry.co.uk.

World Directory of Non-Official Statistical Sources
Gives references to statistics from non-government sources worldwide.
Complementary source: *Sources of Non-Official UK Statistics.*
World Directory of Trade and Business Associations
Gives details of trade and business associations worldwide.
Comparable sources: *Encyclopaedia of Associations: International Organizations, Europa Directory of International Organizations, Yearbook of International Organizations.*
Euromonitor plc, 60–61 Britton Street, London EC1M 5UX. Tel: +44 (0)20 7251 8024. Fax: +44 (0)20 7608 3149. E-mail: info@euromonitor.com. Web: www.euromonitor.com.

World Factbook

Published by the United States Central Intelligence Agency, gives brief profiles of countries and non self-governing territories around the world. Also available online at www.cia.gov/cia/publications/factbook/index.html.

Comparable sources: *Annual Register, Europa World Yearbook, Statesman's Yearbook.*

Available from: Superintendent of Documents, P O Box 371954, Pittsburgh, PA 15250-7954, USA. Tel: +001 202 512 1800. Fax: +001 202 512 2104. Web: http://bookstore.gpo.gov/.

World Marketing Data and Statistics on the Internet

Gives demographic, socio-economic and financial facts and figures for countries worldwide. Also available online.

Euromonitor plc, 60-61 Britton Street, London EC1M 5UX. Tel: +44 (0)20 7251 8024. Fax: +44 (0)20 7608 3149. E-mail: info@euromonitor.com. Web: www.euromonitor.com.

Yearbook of International Organizations

Gives contact details and activities of organizations worldwide. Also available online.

Competitors: *Encyclopaedia of Associations: International Organizations, Europa Directory of International Organizations.*

Comparable sources: *Directory of European Professional and Learned Societies, World Directory of Trade and Business Associations.*

K G Saur Verlag, Ortlerstrasse 8, D-81373 München, Germany. PO Box 70 16 20 81316 München. Tel: +49 (0)89 769020. Fax: +49 (0)89 76902 150. E-mail: saur.info@thomson.com. Web: www.saur.de.

Index

Know It All, Find It Fast

An A-Z source guide for the enquiry desk
Bob Duckett, Peter Walker and Christinea Donnelly

'I wish that I had been able to obtain such a guide when I started dealing with enquiries.' Managing Information

'By the time I got to it 3 staff had noticed it on the desk and written a note saying really good and can we have a copy.' BBOB News

'This is certainly a comforting and very useful guide for the information worker, particularly inexperienced or unqualified, staffing a general enquiry desk.' New Library World

There is a queue, the phone is ringing, the photocopier has jammed and your enquirer is waiting for a response. You are stressed and you can feel the panic rising. Where do you go to find the information you need to answer the question promptly and accurately?

This award-winning sourcebook is an essential guide to where to look to find the answers quickly. It is designed as a first point of reference for library and information practitioners, to be depended upon if they are unfamiliar with the subject of an enquiry – or wish to find out more. It is arranged in an easily searchable, fully cross-referenced A–Z list of around 150 of the subject areas most frequently handled at enquiry desks.

Offering quick and easy pointers to a multitude of information sources, this is an invaluable reference deskbook for all library and information staff in need of a speedy answer, in reference libraries, subject departments and other information units.

2nd edn; 384pp; paperback; 1-85604-534-X; £29.95

The New Walford: Guide to reference resources

Editor-in-chief: Dr Ray Lester

'For a bibliographer caught in between the recent analogue past and entirely digital future of our rapidly developing 'information world' the pleasure of holding this substantial guide to the guides is close to ecstasy. The quality of print and design of the book is remarkable, the paper of high quality, the structure, lay-out and explanations transparent, the possibilities of browsing and searching as good as one can get in the printed reference book.'   Information Research

'Ray Lester and his team of sixteen subject specialists have tackled an enormous job with a refreshing new approach . . . It is an excellent start for the 21st century Walford . . .'   Refer

First published in 1959, *Walford's Guide To Reference Material* achieved international recognition as a leading bibliographic tool across all subject areas. But, in the 1990s, the web transformed the information universe; and so now *Walford* has been transformed.

Published in a 3-volume cycle, *The New Walford* will form the most substantial work of its kind in the English language. The types of material cited have been greatly widened to reflect the revolution brought about by the use of networked information; but print resources are not ignored where these are still valuable.

TNW's new way of categorizing resources reflects the fundamental changes that have taken place in the scientific, business, political and social information landscapes. It will be valuable for information professionals worldwide who need to suggest resources to people who are relatively unfamiliar with the nuances of a topic and who are asking 'where should I start?'

If you are an LIS professional responsible for developing and revising a reference collection, new to reference work, staffing an enquiry desk, a research worker or student, you'll welcome this work – your paper portal to the world of reference resources.

Volume 1: Science, Technology and Medicine
2005; 848pp; hardback; ISBN 1-85604-495-5; £149.95

Look out for Volume 2: The Social Sciences (ISBN 1-85604-498-X) and Volume 3: Arts, Humanities and General Reference (ISBN 1-85604-499-8).